T0358191

Cambridge Elements ☰

Elements in Leadership
edited by
Ronald Riggio
Claremont McKenna College
Susan Murphy
University of Edinburgh
Georgia Sorenson
University of Cambridge

THE HAZARDS OF GREAT LEADERSHIP

Detrimental Consequences of Leader Exceptionalism

James K. Beggan
University of Louisville

Scott T. Allison
University of Richmond

George R. Goethals
University of Richmond

Shaftesbury Road, Cambridge CB2 8EA, United Kingdom

One Liberty Plaza, 20th Floor, New York, NY 10006, USA

477 Williamstown Road, Port Melbourne, VIC 3207, Australia

314–321, 3rd Floor, Plot 3, Splendor Forum, Jasola District Centre,
New Delhi – 110025, India

103 Penang Road, #05–06/07, Visioncrest Commercial, Singapore 238467

Cambridge University Press is part of Cambridge University Press & Assessment,
a department of the University of Cambridge.

We share the University's mission to contribute to society through the pursuit of
education, learning and research at the highest international levels of excellence.

www.cambridge.org
Information on this title: www.cambridge.org/9781009398596

DOI: 10.1017/9781009398589

First published 2023

A catalogue record for this publication is available from the British Library.

ISBN 978-1-009-39859-6 Paperback
ISSN 2631-7796 (online)
ISSN 2631-7788 (print)

The Hazards of Great Leadership

Detrimental Consequences of Leader Exceptionalism

Elements in Leadership

DOI: 10.1017/9781009398589
First published online: April 2023

James K. Beggan
University of Louisville

Scott T. Allison
University of Richmond

George R. Goethals
University of Richmond

Author for correspondence: James K. Beggan, James.beggan@louisville.edu

Abstract: The value of great leaders seems to be an unquestioned assumption. The goal of this Element is to explore the counterintuitive idea that great leaders can pose a hazard to themselves and their followers. Great leadership, which accomplishes morally commendable and difficult objectives by leaders and followers, requires competence, morality, and charisma. A hazard is a condition or event that leads to human loss, such as injury, death, or economic misfortune. A leader can become a hazard through social-psychological processes, which operate through the metaphor of the seven deadly sins to create negative consequences. Great leaders can undermine their own success and accomplishments, as well as those of their followers. They can become a threat to the organization in which they are employed. Finally, great leaders can become a danger to the larger society. The damage great leaders can create can be reduced by applying the corresponding virtue.

Keywords: great leadership, leadership, charisma, seven deadly sins, superstars

ISBNs: 9781009398596 (PB), 9781009398589 (OC)
ISSNs: 2631-7796 (online), 2631-7788 (print)

Contents

Introduction

The value of great leaders seems to be an unquestioned assumption. Just a few minutes of browsing in the business section of a bookstore or scrolling through Amazon.com uncovers texts that promise to define great leadership, identify great leaders, and reveal what traits correlate with great leadership and what behaviors turn someone into a great leader. Many academic and popular press articles identify what attributes distinguish good leaders from great leaders, with the underlying assumption that it is better to be a great leader than a good one.

We make the prima facie assumption that being a leader requires skills and abilities and that, as noted by Festinger (1954, p. 124), "There is a unidirectional drive upward," which would motivate someone to improve their abilities in order to be a better leader. Further, and by extension, we assume that followers and other organization members would appreciate a leader who strives to be exceptional. In other words, an individual will always prefer to be a better leader than one who is less accomplished. Similarly, people prefer to follow a superior rather than lesser leader.

The premise of this Element is that greatness has hidden costs, which people usually overlook. We believe that this blind spot is fundamental to our intuitive beliefs about leadership. In fact, we go so far as to say that the human tendency to see only the benefits of great leadership, while ignoring the hazard of great leadership, represents the *fundamental leadership error*.

The fundamental leadership error involves two related misconceptions. The first is the belief that, regardless of the criteria used to define greatness, it is always better to have a great leader relative to a good one. The second is the assumption that a leader's goodness or greatness stems from their internal characteristics. The name and basis of the fundamental leadership error pay homage to social psychology's *fundamental attribution error*, which describes how people overestimate the role of dispositions – as opposed to situations – in influencing behavior (Ross, 1977). Thomas Carlyle's (1841) great man theory of leadership (now termed "great person theory") is an example of the fundamental error of ascribing dispositional or even genetic greatness to leaders who are probably not deserving of such elevated status.

In a way, this Element saddles the reader with a conundrum. Given the plethora of material devoted to striving to be a better leader and the dearth of books and articles that promise to make their readers *less* accomplished leaders, it would seem counterproductive to argue that in some instances people should *not* strive to become a great leader or that followers should not prefer great leaders. We would never advocate for mediocrity or less-than-effective leadership. However, we do wish to shed light on the hidden hazard of great leadership. Using up-to-date research from leadership studies, psychology, and sociology, we will explain why great leaders, great leadership, or even the quest for great leadership can sometimes lead to harmful consequences for the leaders themselves, their followers and constituents, their organizations and institutions, and larger society as a whole. We will frame our discussion of why these harmful consequences can occur in terms of the seven deadly sins of pride, envy, wrath, sloth, greed, gluttony, and lust, which are often listed in descending order, from the most destructive to the least. In other words, we will explore the counterintuitive idea that there is a hazard posed by great leaders. Much like the warning label on a pack of cigarettes, we caution that great leadership can be hazardous for an organization's health.

Examining the possible downside of great leaders is a novel task. A Google Scholar search for the exact term "great leader" obtained 55,300 hits in October 2022. In contrast, a search for the term "hazard of a great leader" uncovered exactly zero matches and we also found no evidence for variations such as "hazard posed by a great leader." A search on Google revealed similar omissions. A Google search for "great leader" found 15,800,000 hits, whereas "hazard of a great leader" and "downside of great leadership" found zero.

John Emerich Edward Dalberg-Acton, commonly known as Lord Acton, was a nineteenth-century English author, historian, and politician. Although Acton served in the House of Commons and wrote notable political essays, people best remember him for a statement he penned in the Acton–Creighton correspondence, reprinted in the volume *Essays on Freedom and Power*, selected and introduced by Gertrude Himmelfarb and published in 1949: "Power tends to corrupt," wrote Acton, "and absolute power corrupts absolutely" (Acton, 1949, p. 364). In the century and a half since they were written, Acton's words have achieved the status of iconic wisdom, serving as a cautionary tale for any leader holding on to the naïve belief that they are immune to power's nefarious influence.

Often overlooked is the next provocative sentence that Lord Acton wrote in his letter to the bishop: "Great men are almost always bad men." He added, "even when they exercise influence and not authority: still more when you superadd the tendency or the certainty of corruption by authority. There is no worse heresy than that the office sanctifies the holder of it" (p. 364). The "great people are bad people" paradox can be resolved by understanding the human tendency to gravitate toward committing one or more of the *seven deadly sins*. This collection of transgressions was first described by the philosopher and theologian Thomas Aquinas in the thirteenth century. Often listed in descending order, from most destructive to least destructive, the seven sins are *pride*, *envy*, *wrath*, *sloth*, *greed*, *gluttony*, and *lust*.

We consider how human vulnerability to the seven deadly sins – in conjunction with social-psychological processes related to group processes and the relationship between leaders and followers – makes it possible for a great leader to become a hazard to himself or herself, followers, the organization as a whole, and the larger society in which the organization is embedded. These sins can operate on leaders themselves, followers, or even members outside of the organization.

The hazard posed by great leaders is different from destructive leadership. According to Einarsen, Aasland, and Skogstad (2007, p. 208, emphasis in original), *destructive leadership* is defined as "*The systematic and repeated behaviour by a leader, supervisor or manager that violates the legitimate interest of the organisation by undermining and/or sabotaging the organisation's goals, tasks, resources, and effectiveness and/or the motivation, well-being or job satisfaction of subordinates.*" Destructive leadership is often defined by terms such as "abusive supervisors," "bullies," and "toxic leaders."

In contrast, the hazard posed by great leadership is conceptualized as positive behaviors or characteristics that have unintended negative consequences. Leadership, it turns out, is packed with paradox (Bolden, Witzel, & Linacre, 2016). The *Oxford English Dictionary* defines *paradox* as "a seemingly absurd or self-contradictory statement or proposition which when investigated or explained may prove to be well founded or true."[1] Paradoxes are truths that hang upside down to get our attention. Great leaders who ignore the paradoxes of leadership are, by definition, not great leaders and are in fact a hazard to themselves and to their followers.

The most obvious limitation of great leader worship has come clearly into public view through recent revelations about corporate misconduct at the leadership levels. As Fuqua and Newman (2004, pp. 151–152) noted, "Preoccupations with CEOs, their philosophies, personal characteristics, and so forth, reflect a general social attitude in our culture that defers great influence to a very small group of individuals. The full social cost of this model over the past decade is not likely to be realized for several years."

Great leadership can make a positive difference. It helps create positive outcomes on scales both large and small. Ernest Shackleton's leadership of the crew of *Endurance* after it was trapped and crushed in an ice floe off Antarctica in 1915 saved all hands. Against much conventional wisdom, Clara Barton organized women nurses to aid Union soldiers during the American Civil War and became known as the Angel of the Battlefield. Martin Luther King Jr. became the foremost leader of the nonviolent struggle for civil rights for African Americans from 1955

---

[1] https://www.oxfordreference.com/display/10.1093/acref/9780198609810.001.0001/acref-9780198609810-e-5221

until his assassination in 1968. His efforts culminated in the Civil Rights Act of 1964 and the Voting Rights Act of 1965.

Traditional views of leadership have emphasized the importance of individual traits that facilitate someone acting as an influential leader. Other, related approaches recognize that certain behaviors (as opposed to underlying traits that motivate those behaviors) are associated with great leadership. Both of these frameworks implicitly assume that it is always better to have more – rather than less – of a desired attribute.

The *romance of leadership* (Bligh, Kohles, & Pillai, 2011) is an implicit leadership theory (Felfe & Petersen, 2007) that focuses on the tendency to attribute an extensive role to the influence of leaders with regard to the success or failure of an organization (Meindl, Ehrlich, & Dukerich, 1985). Emrich (1999, p. 992) explored people's implicit theories of leadership and noted "numerous studies, all of which indicate that leadership is as much (or more) an idea in the minds of followers as a reality of leaders themselves." As such, the romance of leadership is an "inherently subjectivistic, social constructionist view" (Meindl, 1995, p. 339). According to Meindl, Ehrlich, and Dukerich (1985, p. 79), "It appears that as observers of and as participants in organizations, we may have developed highly romanticized, heroic views of leadership – what leaders do, what they are able to accomplish, and the general effects they have on our lives."

Proponents of the romance of leadership concept have challenged whether leaders have a meaningful effect on organization outcomes. If the leader is seen as successful, people who score high in the tendency to romance leadership are more inclined to approve a project even in the face of information that suggests the likelihood of success is low (Felfe & Petersen, 2007). Although a minority opinion is that leadership does not matter to the success of an organization (Pfeffer, 1977), as noted by Alvesson (2019, p. 39), "the large majority is more or less strongly celebratory of leaders and leadership. Leadership researchers (and practitioners) may have seen too many Hollywood and Disneyland films and/or are too strongly influenced by religion rather than social science."

A number of reasons explain why a belief in the importance of leaders persists. One is that leaders are given credit for success and are blamed for failure, even if their performance is influenced by factors beyond their control, such as economic downturns or historical events. A second reason is that implicit theories of leadership often attribute leaders with the potential for great influence. A third reason is that someone who appears to be a successful leader may be the beneficiary of several instances of good fortune. As such, what is actually luck is interpreted as leadership acumen. Finally, the media tends to romanticize leaders and further contributes to their being perceived as important influences.

One consequence of distinguishing between leader and follower roles is that among followers, as noted by Einola and Alvesson (2021, p. 856), "The follower role is embraced as limited, narrow and subordinated to the leader in terms of initiative, responsibility, influencing and work activity. There is little thinking about the entire picture." As such, they suggest that "leadership may be a double-edged sword, where trust in leadership may simultaneously trigger respect and good relations as well as processes of immaturization" (p. 860). In other words, trust in a great leader – mediated by the deadly sin of sloth – may make followers – like children – less hardworking and less ambitious.

Skepticism about leader effectiveness can take two forms. In one instance, it is possible that, although leaders do influence organizational outcomes, the inherent superiority of one leader in comparison to another will be overrated. The strong, and more controversial, form challenges the notion that leaders have any influence at all on organizational outcomes.

One reason that the identity of a specific leader may not be important is that leaders and their impact are effectively more homogeneous than might initially be assumed. One explanation is that leaders typically self-select to assume or be nominated for a leadership role. As such, there may be a restricted range of candidates (with a corresponding limited range of attributes) to take on a leadership role. Further, constraints on leaders may limit their range of possible behaviors. These constraints may be internal and stem from within the organization; they may also be external and can include government regulations as well as the perspectives of opinion leaders. Leaders can also vary in the degree they tailor their leadership style to the needs of individual followers, i.e., are they heterogeneous or homogeneous in their treatment of followers (Klein & House, 1995)?

The very belief in the concept of a great leader can interfere with the quality of leadership by reducing the perceived value of leader development. Almost by definition, great leaders do not require further training or education. Additionally, a belief in great leadership can undermine the potential effectiveness of someone who is merely good. In other words, with leadership, it is important to avoid letting the search for the great be the enemy of satisfaction with the good.

1 The Challenge of Defining "Greatness"

To explore the hazard posed by a great leader, we need to define what we mean by both a great leader and a hazard. Defining a great leader is not an easy task. As noted by Horner (1997, p. 275), "Is there a clear, single profile that exists for a great leader? Most likely there is not." For example, Al-Nasour and Najm (2020) identified six elements of excellent leadership: possessing a strategic vision, influencing others, serving as a moral role model, maintaining external relations, achieving business success, and developing pathways for future leaders to emerge. One problem of being a great leader is that it may require balancing competing or contradictory goals or attributes. For example, outstanding leadership can be viewed in terms of possessing both humility and fierce resolve (Xu et al., 2019). The paradox of authentic leadership involves the trade-off between matching words and deeds and appearing relatable (Goffee & Jones, 2005).

The belief in great leaders is associated with the ongoing debate over whether great leaders are "born" or "made." The innate approach was advocated by Carlyle (1841) in his "great person" explanation for heroism. Carlyle argued that certain individuals possessed qualities such as intelligence, wisdom, and goodness that made them destined for greatness (Spector, 2016). The disparity between the income earned by the average employee and a CEO is consistent with implicit beliefs in a great person theory of leadership (Koehn, 2014).

According to an analysis by von Hippel (2018), income disparities are *not* caused by disparities in innate abilities but are rather the result of beliefs about innate disparities in abilities. When the gap between the rich and the poor first appeared, people psychologically justified the gap by judging the rich to be inherently superior to the poor. A belief that greatness is innate also fits with an essentialist approach that minimizes the role of socialization and prior experience in developing exceptional leaders. Certain disciplines such as sociology tend to be hostile to essentialist approaches because people view them as reifying class and status differences (Fuchs, 2001).

Greatness in leadership must surely involve the wisdom to map out highly challenging ethical goals and ethical means to achieve them. Moreover, leaders must be able to persuade followers and mobilize them to act toward those goals. Thus, we define a great leader in terms of the three dimensions of competence, morality, and charisma. Competence is required to achieve a goal. Morality is necessary to ensure that the goals sought achieve the greater good. Charisma is needed because leaders must be able to motivate others – followers – to work toward the vision described by a leader. These three dimensions are distinct but correlated. Our definition of greatness builds on work relevant to understanding heroism. Virtue and competence are core dimensions of heroism (Allison & Goethals, 2011; Goethals & Allison, 2012). Charisma is an important attribute of heroism, and although fame is not necessary to define someone as heroic (Goethals & Allison, in press), it is often the case that heroes become famous.

Many studies of leadership show that good leadership is associated with having a particular personality profile along the five dimensions of the Big Five personality traits (Costa & McCrae, 1992). The five factors are often referred to by the acronym OCEAN, with each letter representing, in turn, openness to experience, conscientiousness, extraversion, agreeableness, and neuroticism. Openness to experience is sometimes referred to as intellect and is related to knowing and being open enough to make good decisions. Conscientiousness supports self-regulation and therefore ethical behavior. Conscientiousness and agreeableness are related to ethical leadership (Kalshoven, Den Hartog, & De Hoogh, 2011). Extraversion and agreeableness contribute to being willing and able to engage with potential followers. With neuroticism, a low score indicates high emotional stability, predicting good leadership. Stability (the absence of neuroticism) helps with perseverance and steadiness of emotional outlook during stressful leadership moments. It helps great leaders keep on an even keel.

In one extension of the Big Five literature, the HEXACO model of personality adds an honesty–humility dimension, which includes qualities such as modesty, sincerity, fairness, and avoiding greed (Ashton & Lee, 2007). This added dimension supports ethical behavior and effective interaction with potential followers.

Great leadership is the accomplishment of morally commendable and difficult objectives by leaders and their followers. In other words, great leadership is accomplished by possessing and acting in accord with the opposite traits of the seven deadly sins. Traits such as humility, conscientiousness, and agreeableness are counterpoints to sins like pride, wrath, greed, and sloth.

While there can be endless hair-splitting debate about whether things done by past leaders and followers were exceedingly difficult or entirely ethical, we are confident that we can identify examples of leaders who fully meet the standards of morality and competence. Jimmy Carter's leadership in producing the Camp David Accords between the United States, Egypt, and Israel in 1978 can be considered an example of great leadership, even if Carter's overall performance as president is not considered great. At the time, the Israeli prime minister Menachem Begin said that Carter had "worked harder than our forefathers did in Egypt in building the pyramids." That agreement, despite numerous challenges, has resulted in peace between Israel and Egypt for more than forty years.

Leadership Mismatches

Defining great leadership as both effective and ethical raises questions about how we should regard leadership that is effective but not ethical or ethical but not effective. Should we call effective, competent leadership that accomplishes immoral or unethical goals "great leadership?" We contend that great leadership requires the *accomplishment* of difficult goals. The prominent leadership scholar James MacGregor Burns wrote that leadership is "*measured by the degree of production of intended effects*" and that the test of "leadership is the degree of *actual accomplishment* of the promised change" (Burns, 1978, p. 22, emphasis in original).

We need also to ask whether cases in which a leader and some followers make heroic efforts for a moral cause against great odds but fail to accomplish their goals constitute great leadership. Such leadership is ethical but not effective. Families of children and teenagers killed in school shootings have mobilized to achieve the banning of assault weapons, a goal most Americans think makes sense, but they have not succeeded.

Franco (2017) has argued that "heroic failure" is *not* a failed effort to show great leadership. Rather, it is not making any effort at all. Bystanders who do nothing to help someone in an emergency are showing both failed leadership and heroic failure. For this reason, the heroism activist Matt Langdon has said that the opposite of a "hero" is not a "villain"; it is a bystander. Leadership, and great leadership in particular, is an activity, not a silent intention.

In examining great leadership, it is helpful to understand its opposite, namely bad leadership. In her aptly named book *Bad Leadership*, Barbara Kellerman (2004) discusses three types of ineffective leadership and four types of unethical leadership. Ineffective leadership includes the categories of incompetent, rigid, and intemperate. Unethical leadership types include callous, corrupt, insular, and evil. These categories certainly map onto the seven deadly sins.

Effective leadership, especially great leadership, generally requires the antithesis of all three kinds of ineffective leadership. Leading greatly demands competence, flexibility, and self-control. Great leadership in wartime often illustrates exceptionally effective leadership marked by those three qualities. Although great leadership is associated with the opposite of the seven deadly sins, as we will show, the temptation produced by the seven deadly sins can influence leaders and followers to act in ways that undermine leadership effectiveness. Further, the abilities and opportunities afforded by great leadership may make it easier for the seven deadly sins to do their malevolent work.

Kellerman's typology of unethical leadership suggests that morally commendable leadership must be honest rather than corrupt, caring of followers rather than callous, and mindful of the greater good as well as the needs of the in-group. Being ethically or morally commendable in all of these ways is a tall order. For example, sometimes what is good for one's followers, the in-group, does not benefit the greater good. Kellerman offers the example of President Bill Clinton's nonintervention into the Rwanda genocide as immoral leadership because it was, in her terms, insular. Yet nonintervention arguably saved American lives. But leadership that is ethical on all four dimensions does happen. Clara Barton's leadership noted in the Introduction was clearly ethical: honest, caring, helpful to humanity generally and not just her followers, and the opposite of evil. And it qualifies as great leadership because it was effective as well as ethical.

The Morality of Great Leaders

It is possible to distinguish between a descriptive and normative definition of morality (Gert & Gert, 2020). A descriptive definition focuses on codes of conduct that people actually live by; in contrast, a normative definition focuses on codes of conduct that would be advanced by rational people with regard to how they should live their lives. Different groups can put forward distinct and sometimes incompatible codes of conduct (Luco, 2014). Great leaders possess the acumen to navigate these differences.

There are five foundational concerns for morality (Graham et al., 2013). These involve the well-being of others, fairness, loyalty to one's group, respect for the social order and hierarchical relationships, and concerns about physical and spiritual purity. The political left in the United States tends to value the first two of these moral foundations (well-being and fairness), whereas the political right tends to value all five. Great leaders find a way to value, empower, and unite both ends of the spectrum. The sins of envy and wrath are clearly opposed to encouraging the well-being of others.

McGuire (1973) suggested that the opposite of a great truth is also a great truth. Similarly, it is possible that the opposite of a virtue is an opposing virtue (as opposed to a vice). A virtue conflict operates when the pursuit of one virtue may conflict with the ability to satisfy an alternative virtue (Grant & Schwartz, 2011). As noted by Allison and Goethals (2016), countries wage war against each other, with each side proclaiming the moral upper hand. Great leaders help their followers balance the rich complexity and paradoxical nature of moral differences among their constituents.

The Competence of Great Leaders

Broadly defined, *competence* refers to an individual's ability to interact effectively with the environment (White, 1959). Effective leadership involves the ability to motivate and coordinate followers to complete tasks, to achieve performance goals, and to mediate between an organization and the larger environment. Leader competence involves intelligence, decisiveness, being hardworking, and possessing the relevant qualifications (Sturm, Vera, & Crossan, 2017). Leaders can possess competencies across cognitive, emotional, or social domains (Boyatzis, 2011). Sins such as sloth and gluttony operate in direct opposition to attributes that would lead to competence. Specific leader attributes may be more effective in one setting in comparison to another (Peters, Hartke, & Pohlmann, 1985).

Great leadership certainly depends on intelligence that is relevant to the challenges leaders face in mobilizing followers and the challenges leaders and followers face together in accomplishing their common goals. Two important perspectives on intelligence are helpful in understanding the role of intelligence. Horn and Cattell (1966) distinguished between fluid and crystallized intelligence. *Fluid* intelligence is the ability to reason and process information, as well as the capacity to learn new things. *Crystallized* intelligence is what we have learned and what we know from our experience.

In his book *The Mask of Command*, the military historian John Keegan (1987) describes knowing and seeing as crucial to wise action in battle. Knowing is essentially crystallized intelligence about factors such as the physical landscape, resources available to both one's own forces and the enemy's, and the personal qualities and capacities of enemy commanders and their forces. Seeing is the ability to take in what is happening in the moment on the field of battle and make good decisions based on the unfolding events. It clearly involves fluid intelligence that uses the relevant knowledge or crystallized intelligence. Great leadership depends on the intelligence to make good decisions, both in planning and in adapting as events evolve. Both crystallized and fluid intelligence are traits needed for great leadership.

A second perspective on intelligence that helps understand how cognitive capacities support competent leadership comes from Howard Gardner's (1983) *Frames of Mind: The Theory of Multiple Intelligences*. Gardner (1993, p. 6) views intelligence as associated with "the ability to solve problems, or fashion products that are of consequence in a particular cultural setting or community." For us, it is a leader's capacity to find solutions to difficult challenges facing followers in specific situations.

Recent research finds that decision-making competence, certainly a quality key to competent leadership, depends on motivation and emotion regulation (Bruine de Bruin, Parker, & Fischhoff, 2020). Motivation and emotional regulation involve self-awareness, self-regulation, motivation, empathy, and social skills (Reeves, 2005). They also require perceiving, understanding, using, and managing emotions, both in oneself and in others (Salovey & Grewal, 2005). Thus, leader effectiveness depends on the ability to regulate oneself, including the ability to maintain high levels of motivation, as well as the ability to perceive oneself and others accurately and with enough understanding of followers' emotions to use emotional appeals to engage and mobilize them.

We suggest that being too competent – defined in terms of intelligence, decisiveness, emotional regulation, and being hardworking – can, paradoxically, ultimately interfere with leadership effectiveness. A highly competent or successful leader can create "immaturation of followers" (Einola & Alvesson, 2021, p. 846). Simonton (1985) proposed several models to describe a nonlinear relationship between intelligence and success. It is possible that being too smart can be detrimental to a leader's effectiveness (Antonakis, House, & Simonton, 2017). Possible reasons are that their solutions to problems may be too sophisticated, they use language that is too complex, or they fail to meet the prototypic image of a leader or of a leader for the particular group they represent.

In the domain of leadership, competence is a dimension that may produce negative returns if it operates in conjunction with a reduction in follower motivation. In other words, leader competence can create follower sloth. Employees may exert less effort if they believe that their leader will change their work or can do the work better. This hypothesized process is similar to what operates for *social loafing*, where the presence of other actors can reduce motivation and effort on collective tasks (Karau & Williams, 1993). *Servant leadership*, a style where the leader focuses on follower growth and development (van Dierendonck, 2011), is the opposite of pride and is effective in reducing social loafing (Stouten & Liden, 2020). As such, it is possible that different manifestations of great leadership – as a selfless inspiration or as a high-achieving superstar – may differentially influence follower motivation.

One factor that can undermine leader effectiveness is when leaders' own ambition – their pride and greed – puts them at odds with the well-being of their employees, the organization, or the larger community in which the organization exists. They may be poor listeners, dislike mentoring, and be too sensitive to negative feedback. Finally, they may encourage their followers to engage in *groupthink*, a style of group decision-making that reduces creativity and personal responsibility (Park, 2000).

The Charisma of Great Leaders

In the *Oxford English Dictionary*, the two definitions of charisma are "compelling attractiveness or charm that can inspire devotion in others" and "divinely conferred power or talent."[2] According to Barnes (1978, p. 1), the sociologist Max Weber defined charisma as a "certain quality of an individual's personality, by virtue of which he is set apart from ordinary men and treated as endowed with supernatural, superhuman, or at least specifically exceptional powers or qualities." Exceptional levels of charisma may increase the likelihood that a leader would be prideful or gluttonous.

---

[2] *Oxford English Dictionary*, s.v. "Charisma." https://www.oxfordreference.com/display/10.1093/acref/9780198609810.001.0001/acref-9780198609810-e-5221;jsessionid=7C28B03ABC28B38081 2FFC5AEDFE6210 (accessed 17 February 2023).

Attempting to define a charismatic leader can be difficult (Antonakis et al., 2016) and the term is often left undefined, poorly defined, or tautologically defined (Antonakis, 2017). Just as Goethals and Allison (2012, p. 186) stated that "heroism is in the eye of the beholder," it is also the case that "charisma is in the eye of the beholder" (Callan, 2003, p. 10). One way to define charisma in leadership studies is as a specific set of traits (Riggio, 1998), such as emotional expressiveness, enthusiasm, drive, eloquence, self-confidence, responsiveness to others, and being visionary. According to Shamir (1992, p. 388), "charismatic leaders . . . are commonly perceived by their followers as 'larger than life' and as having extraordinary influence on events."

According to House and Baetz (1979, p. 399), charismatic leaders "by the force of their personal abilities are capable of having profound and extraordinary effects on followers." Conger and Kanungo (1987) differentiated between charismatic and noncharismatic leaders along several dimensions. Among those dimensions were an opposition to the status quo and a motivation to change it, expertise in using unconventional methods to achieve their goals, a strong articulation of a future vision, and adopting an elitist orientation geared toward transforming people to share in a vision in support of the radical changes.

Although competence can be distinguished conceptually from charisma or *fame*, which refers to being known to people whom you do not know (Greenberg et al., 2010), great success can lead to prominence. It is also possible that people will assume famous people are competent as an extension of a *halo effect*, "generally defined as the influence of a global evaluation on evaluations of individual attributes of a person" (Nisbett & Wilson, 1977, p. 250), which operates for favorable and unfavorable information. Fame can be an important goal even in disciplines that would seem disinterested in celebrity, such as science (Chan, Mixon, & Torgler, 2019). Moreover, the pursuit of fame in and of itself, as opposed to as a byproduct of accomplishment, has become a more important motivation in and of itself in modern society (Cowen, 2000). The desire for fame could be viewed as a manifestation of pride, envy, greed, and gluttony.

Charismatic leaders use a number of behavioral strategies (Ehrhart & Klein, 2001). They communicate high expectations for performance, express the belief that their followers can achieve their goals, take risks in order to challenge the status quo, and put forward a value-based vision and collective identity. Self-sacrifice can promote the perception that someone is a charismatic leader (de Cremer & van Knippenberg, 2002).

As a leadership trait, charisma's effect may operate in the shape of an inverted "U." A leader who lacks charisma may only achieve a mundane level of success. As charisma increases, leader effectiveness increases. After a certain point, charisma may interfere with effective leadership. Although charismatic leaders can promote cooperation (de Cremer & van Knippenberg, 2002), they have also been criticized (Tilstra, 2010). Charismatic leaders may be grandiose, exploitative, and self-promoting, i.e., prideful, greedy, and perhaps possessing the capacity for wrath. Further, they may promote passivity, i.e., slothfulness, in followers.

Great Leader vs. Great Leadership

There is a distinction between great leadership and a great leader. To say someone is a leader, especially to call them a great leader, puts them in a distinct category with all kinds of associations. Culturally, we have a leader prototype, most likely based on an unconscious leader archetype (Simonton, 1987), that includes assumptions about a leader's personal qualities. This prototype contains beliefs that a great leader is strong, active, and good. In his book *Blink*, Malcolm Gladwell (2005) identified the *Warren Harding error*. Because Harding was very handsome and had a "sonorous" voice, his advisors, as well as the majority of the American people in the presidential election of 1920, thought he looked like a president. Despite his presidential appearance, experts rate Harding as one of the worst presidents ever.

A person performing a single feat of great leadership may or may not have those qualities or may not exhibit them consistently. Many people (e.g., Last, 2022) believe that the former US vice president Mike Pence performed an act of heroic leadership on January 6, 2021, when he refused to succumb to pressure from the former president Donald Trump to overthrow the 2020 presidential election. Others (e.g., Shafer, 2022) argue that he went along with Trump's efforts to overthrow the election up until the very end. As such, he would not be considered a hero (Cillizza, 2022). However, even if Pence performed an act of great leadership, one might not say he was a great leader. Rather, he could be viewed as a hero for one day, not one for all seasons.

In distinguishing great leadership from great leaders, two closely related cognitive biases may easily transform instances of great leadership into perceptions of the leader as a great leader and perhaps even a hero. First is Meindl's (1995) idea of the romance of leadership, our tendency to see leadership as the cause of good or bad group outcomes, particularly group success or failure, and to overlook other factors that explain at least in part the group's outcome. Poor leadership is taken as the explanation for the organization's failure. When sports teams do badly, the coach is often fired. Consider, for example, Joshua Lawrence Chamberlain's great leadership on Little Round Top during the battle at Gettysburg in 1863. At a desperate moment, when his Twentieth Maine

Regiment had run out of ammunition, Chamberlain ordered the downhill bayonet charge that saved the day; however, there were multiple influences on the way it turned out. For example, the Confederate forces trying to overwhelm his position were themselves overwhelmed by thirst and fatigue on a blisteringly hot July afternoon.

Another cognitive bias that operates on judgments of great leadership is one that we mentioned earlier, namely the tendency to attribute a person's behavior to dispositions or traits rather than situational factors. This tendency, often called the *fundamental attribution error*, can be viewed as a *correspondence bias* where an underlying trait is assumed to correspond with a parallel action (Gilbert & Malone, 1995). We routinely attribute behavior to personal qualities because, as the great psychologist Fritz Heider (1958, p. 54) wrote, "behavior in particular has such salient properties it tends to engulf the total field rather than be confined to its proper position as a local stimulus." We might think of brave and decisive action, such as what Chamberlain exhibited on Little Round Top, as corresponding to and being explained by the leader's personal decisiveness and courage. Doing so ignores the fact that he could plainly see that there was no other choice. We credit him for seeing that, but his ability to do so does not mean in itself that he was a great leader.

People's attributes can influence the degree to which they are viewed as possessing the traits of a leader, even if those traits are not relevant to their actual competence, morality, or charisma. One important characteristic that affects others' judgment of a person is physical attractiveness. Important work, beginning with a study by Dion, Berscheid, and Walster (1972, p. 285), has demonstrated a *beauty bias* that assumes "what is beautiful is good." Attractiveness can even influence the perceived moral standing of animals (Klebl et al., 2021). Because we tend to think of attractive people as having other valued personal characteristics, we might think of them as good leaders. The effect of attractiveness on judgment is largest for social competence, moderate for intellectual competence and effectiveness, and close to zero for integrity and concern for others (Eagly et al., 1991). As such, attractive people may be thought of as great leaders if the basis for their leadership role is social or intellectual competence.

The relationship between attractiveness and morality is complex (Han & Laurent, 2023). If attractiveness is associated with vanity, then people may be viewed as less moral if they are attractive. Similarly, an attractive woman was judged more harshly if she engaged in premarital intercourse relative to an unattractive woman (Hocking, Walker, & Fink, 1982). Appearing strong and impressively large can lead to perceptions that an individual is a good leader. George Washington's size (he was much taller than average) and his graceful movement and controlled demeanor made an impact on followers (Brookhiser, 1996). They liked what they saw. Brookhiser (1996, p. 55) makes the general point that "rulers who are intelligent, prudent, or visionary must make a sensual impact if they are to lead. If their bodies cannot command attention, they must compel it by secondary means, such as by eloquence, or by props."

Motional intelligence is the idea that people can impress others by the way they move. During televised debates, the way political figures move and carry themselves can have an effect on the audience's favorability judgments (Fein, Goethals, & Kugler, 2007; Goethals, 2005). Motional variables and other variables related to appearance have long been credited with favoring Kennedy over Nixon in their televised debates (Kraus, 1996). Kennedy's demeanor and mannerisms, cues not available to radio listeners, conveyed great self-assurance while Nixon appeared ill at ease and insecure. With regard to the Kennedy–Nixon debates, others have disagreed and called the distinction in perceptions of viewers and listeners a myth (Vancil & Pendell, 1987). What appeared to be Nixon's advantage with radio audiences might have been produced by a bias toward Republican listeners (Bruschke & Divine, 2017). However, experimental research using the broadcasts as stimulus materials has demonstrated that perceivers use the televised images to form impressions of Kennedy and Nixon, such that television viewers were more influenced by candidate image (such as integrity) and radio listeners relied on issues (Druckman, 2003).

Great leaders are thought to possess charisma. In some cases, people are perceived as charismatic if they possess certain superficial traits. An analysis of speeches by Steve Jobs (Niebuhr, Voße, & Brem, 2016) suggested that variation and variety are key contributors to being viewed as charismatic. Even though they are no smarter, people who answer questions quickly are seen as more charismatic by their friends (von Hippel et al., 2016).

With regard to the potential hazard represented by great leaders and great leadership, charisma is an example of a single dimension that displays a parabolic utility function (Vergauwe et al., 2018). A leader who lacks charisma may be ineffective because he or she lacks a strategic vision. At some optimal level, leader effectiveness reaches a peak. Beyond this peak, increasing charisma may decrease a leader's effectiveness by making him or her less attentive to day-to-day operational duties. Further, a high level of charisma may transform an effective leader into a cult figure (Strong & Killingsworth, 2011).

Is great leadership real or just something that followers or other observers attribute to people in specific situations? Whether there is such a thing as "a great leader" apart from perceptions and attributions is less clear. Few would say that Jimmy Carter was a great leader. Too many times he failed to achieve his goals, and those failures were in part due to personal qualities that made it difficult for him to get others to go along with his decisions. Furthermore, very seldom did the way he act, or the results that ensued from those actions, activate a "great leader" prototype or schema. However, even though we think great leadership must be distinguished from the idea of the great leader, and even though personal qualities are only part of the explanation for how successful leaders act, it is important to recognize that personal characteristics explain in significant measure what leaders do, how they do it, and how well it works.

Researchers have long framed attitude change as the study of who says what to whom with what effect. Persuasion happens when the qualities of a messenger and a message combine to induce potential followers to pay attention to, understand, and accept what the leader says or writes. Does the aspiring leader have the personal qualities – looks, voice, stage presence – to draw attention? Do leaders' words and the way they are spoken or written – in person or through a medium of writing, radio, television, film or the Internet – create understanding and acceptance? Both the message and the messenger are important. Both the leader's persona and his or her message must match to some degree what followers need and expect from the leader, and the leader's message must fit with what followers are prepared to pay attention to, comprehend, and accept.

Commanding attention is aided by the kinds of salient attributes discussed earlier: sensual impact from good looks, compelling voice, or other aspects of charisma. Those same qualities can make an audience open to a message. Then, the message and the way it is delivered, both the "words and music" so to speak, must be engaging and comprehensible to potential followers. Finally, the words themselves have to at least sound or seem sensible.

2 Defining a Hazard

A *hazard* is a condition or event that leads to human loss, such as injury, death, or economic misfortune (Smith, 2013). A hazard is distinct from the damage it can cause. Leaders can operate as hazards because they and their followers can fall victim to the deleterious influence of the seven deadly sins.

As an extreme example of a hazard, consider an asteroid that comes uncomfortably close to the earth. It is a hazard, but as long as it does not actually hit the earth, it causes no damage. If it does hit, however, the negative consequences include earthquakes, volcanic activity, tidal waves, extreme heat, and dust in the air that blocks sunlight and results in the inability of plants to carry out photosynthesis. These consequences will lead to the mass extinction of animal life. Of course, in the asteroid example, there are no positive outcomes. In the very long term, hazards may cause some benefits. Clearly, this is from the point of view of three human beings writing a book about leadership. The rise of mammals – and ultimately human beings – was due in part to the extinction of dinosaurs caused by an asteroid that created the 125-mile-wide Chicxulub impact crater beneath the Gulf of Mexico. It was not so great for the dinosaurs.

A hazard can be conceptualized along a number of dimensions (Gravley, 2001). Magnitude refers to how much impact a hazard could have on human welfare. Frequency refers to how often the hazard occurs or becomes a risk. Duration refers to how long an event remains a threat. Area of extent refers to how much of an organization could be affected; similarly, spatial dispersion refers to whether the potential impact of the hazard differs from one location to another. These dimensions apply to the potential influence of a malevolent leader, who could be viewed as a hazard. A selfish or incompetent leader can potentially do harm to himself or herself, his or her followers and constituents, the organization as a whole, and the larger society in which the organization and the people in the organization operate. The contribution of this Element is to argue that a well-intended or even quite accomplished leader can also become a hazard. The potential hazard posed by an exceptional leader is even more nefarious because cultural scripts and expectations about great leaders do not include the notion that they can cause harm. One hazard similarly shared by both nefarious and noble leaders is the potential influence of the seven deadly sins on their potential legacy as leaders. The difference is that malevolent leaders may happily embrace their corruption whereas well-intended leaders are lured into self-serving actions.

Risk analysis involves assessing the degree of risk to human life and property associated with the presence of a hazard. Risk analysis involves answering three questions (Kaplan & Garrick, 1981). The first concerns what can happen, i.e., what elements are contained in the set of possible events. The second involves the likelihood that each possible event will occur. The third considers the consequences of the event should it occur. Implicit in risk analysis is the assumption that the consequences of the event are negative.

In the decision-making literature, *risk* is defined differently and focuses on situations where an individual has accurate knowledge of the probability distribution associated with a set of outcomes (Milburn & Billings, 1976). The roll of the dice is a risk with a calculable probability. In contrast, *uncertainty* exists for situations where probabilities cannot be assigned to outcomes. Whether lightning will strike a given house is an uncertain probability.

A *disaster* occurs when the potential risk created by a hazard is realized. It is possible to conceptualize a disaster in terms of the physical dimensions of the event, the social and societal consequences, and the symbolic meaning the event may possess (Kroll-Smith, Couch, & Couch, 1991). Natural disasters (such as earthquakes and floods) would be beyond the ability of anyone to prevent; however, leadership can come into play with regard to preemptive responses to a potential crisis, as well as the way leadership handles the subsequent reaction. A recent example of leadership failure in the case of a naturally occurring disaster is the 2021 Texas power market catastrophe in response to the huge power outage during Winter Storm Uri (Rubin, 2021). Although the cold weather could not be prevented, the mechanical failure of the Texas natural gas system, which was used to provide power, could have been avoided had the pipelines and wells been properly winterized (Langford, 2022). Similarly, with the *Challenger* shuttle disaster record low temperatures reduced the effectiveness of the O-rings; however, the failure of the O-rings could be traced to the poor engineering practices of the company that manufactured them, as well as management insistence that the launch occur in spite of protests from engineers (Vaughan, 1996).

In both cases, cold weather was a hazard, which created a risk for human beings going about their day-to-day activities. The disasters occurred because of a complex set of circumstances and failures of leadership. Some aspects of leadership could also be viewed as hazards in their own right. With regard to the Texas power crisis, Republican leaders blamed the disaster on irrelevant factors such as the Green New Deal and windmills (Waldman, 2021) rather than focus on efforts to resolve the problem for the future. In other words, politicking was a hazard to the safety of Texas citizens. With regard to the *Challenger* and the weather crisis in Texas, poor leadership, carried out by poor leaders, can be viewed as one culprit for why the disasters occurred. It is not surprising that poor leaders would do a poor job, which would leave open a door to disaster. In other words, it is easy to conceptualize poor leaders as hazards.

It is perhaps more surprising to argue that great leaders – who presumably carry out great leadership – might also be classified as hazards. We generally accept that leaders vary in their ability to contribute meaningfully to the smooth functioning of an organization or the well-being of employees. As such, a specific leader or type of leader could represent a hazard to the extent that he or she interferes with institutional effectiveness. On the other hand, most people would expect that a great leader – almost by definition – would not be a hazard and would be, in fact, a safeguard. Instead, we suggest that great leaders themselves are a hazard that can increase the risk of disaster. The likelihood of these negative outcomes is reasonably plausible, and the consequences involve harm to the organization, the people who make up the organization, and the larger society as a whole.

Too Much of a Good Thing

According to White (2004, p. 189, footnote), "In its basic form utility can be defined as the balance of pain over pleasure; however . . . pain and pleasure need not just involve physical sensations. Perhaps a better definition would be the balance of interests advanced over those hindered." From a utility perspective, a leader's utility would correspond to the balance between the benefits a leader provides measured against the costs extracted by his or her leadership.

One way to conceptualize a leader's influence is as a utility function, such that a higher level of leader ability leads to an increasing level of leader utility, i.e., better leaders are more useful. Organizational effectiveness – measured with indicators such as productivity, profits, or employee satisfaction – can represent proxies for leader utility. A simple linear function would mean that leader ability and leader utility would increase to infinity. More realistically, however, even if leader ability is positively associated with leader utility, as leader ability increases, leader utility will display a negatively accelerated growth curve. That is, an increasing level of leader ability will be associated with an increasing level of utility; however, the amount of increase in utility will become smaller. In other words, after a certain point, leadership utility will plateau regardless of increasing leader ability.

Alternatively, it is possible that as leader ability increases beyond a certain point, leader utility will actually decrease in response. In other words, the relationship between leader ability and leader utility fits a parabolic, inverted U-shaped function. A classic example of such a non-monotonic function is the Yerkes–Dodson curve (Corbett, 2015), which describes the relationship between arousal and task performance. Thus, great leaders may have a paradoxical and negative effect on organizational effectiveness such that the optimality of leader ability can be best understood as a single-peaked preference (Coombs & Avrunin, 1977). One goal of our work is to present examples where increasing a leader trait beyond a certain point will ultimately reduce leader effectiveness.

There are two ways to create a single-peaked preference. One would hypothesize that, beyond a certain point, leadership ability begins to have a toxic effect on leader utility. Negative and positive effects can emerge from the same action (Grant & Schwartz, 2011). Further, the relative sizes and ranges of operation for these effects can differ from one situation to another or from one person to the next. An example of this is how the effects of alcohol change as a function of its concentration in the body. At a very low level, alcohol has no noticeable impact. As blood-alcohol content increases, a person tends to feel less anxious, more relaxed, and more confident. After a certain point, however, relaxation becomes lethargy and confidence becomes recklessness. As blood-alcohol content increases even more, a person will begin to feel sick and could potentially die from alcohol poisoning. In the case of alcohol, a very different effect results from different levels of concentration of the same substance. As noted by Coombs and Avrunin (1977, p. 224), as a general rule "good things satiate and bad things escalate." In other words, the magnitude of the positive effect goes down even as the potential for sickness moves toward the possibility of death.

Polarization refers to increasingly extreme positions. Leaders can increase polarization for a number of reasons (McCoy & Somer, 2021). In some instances, leaders will encourage polarization in order to satisfy ideological goals, such as what occurred with Martin Luther King Jr. and the civil rights movement. In other, less-well-intended instances, leaders will encourage polarization in order to fulfill opportunistic goals related to attributes such as pride, envy, wrath, and greed. Polarization can spiral out of control due to self-reinforcing social and psychological processes that drive people further apart. Given that in-group favoritism can operate without awareness on the part of social judges (Rudman, Feinberg, & Fairchild, 2002), polarization can also occur without conscious effort on the part of a leader through psychological processes that lead to in-group favoritism (Kershaw et al., 2021).

Another way to hypothesize how leader ability and utility can operate as an inverted U is to note that a separate factor could operate in an antagonistic fashion and offset the increasing effect on leader utility produced by an increasing level of leader ability. For example, a highly adept leader may be asked to make public appearances, write books, or join professional organizations. These additional demands could cause a leader to spend less time actually working as a leader.

It is clear that leaders can take advantage of their authority to engage in self-serving behavior for themselves or the organizations they lead (Rus, van Knippenberg, & Wisse, 2010). Letters to shareholders tend to explain negative performance in a self-serving way in terms of external factors (Staw, McKechnie, & Puffer, 1983). Even attributes or actions that are not illegal, such as excessive executive compensation, can reduce follower loyalty and increase maladjusted behavior within an organization (Bok, 1993).

Alternatively, it is possible that a characteristic that is not harmful in itself will become harmful in conjunction with another factor. Money is perhaps the most obvious commodity thought to have a monotonic value. For example, in a paper on monotonicity and regret theory, Loomes, Starmer, and Sugden (1992, p. 17) wrote, "more money is preferred to less under certainty – something that we shall assume throughout this paper." The underlying assumption of this quote is that more money is always better than less money. Although a seemingly reasonable assumption, it is important to recognize that people may not always treat more money as an addition in value; these seemingly inconsistent findings come into play in the discipline of behavioral economics (Thaler, 2017). Under this assumption, as money increases so does some other quantity, such as satisfaction or a sense of security.

In the classic novel *Stranger in a Strange Land* (Heinlein, 1961, p. 211, emphasis in original), the wise Jubal Harshaw says, "you don't *know* what an Old Man of the Sea great wealth is. Its owner finds himself beset on every side ... He becomes suspicious – honest friendship is rarely offered him ... Worse yet, his family is always in danger." This quote captures a sentiment that wealth should not be thought of as a monotonically increasing function because great wealth creates a new set of problems caused by a new factor, i.e., the threats posed by criminals, grifters, and opportunists.

The Dangers of Superstars

Superstars tend to be people who possess an exceptional degree of talent or popularity (Brandes, Franck, & Nüesch, 2008). In other instances, superstars may not possess greater talent; instead, their exceptional value may result from their fame, i.e., more people knowing about them (Adler, 1985). According to Mullin and Dunn (2002, p. 621), "Star quality thus consists of both reputation based on past performance and charisma above and beyond actual playing ability." Superstars are most likely in entertainment; certain factors, such as the uniqueness of each match, may limit but not erase superstar effects in sports (Lucifora & Simmons, 2003).

A superstar earns a disproportionate amount of money and dominates the activities in which he or she engages (Rosen, 1981). Superstars are valued by an organization because they can have a positive effect on revenue (Hausman & Leonard, 1997), prestige (McCurdy & Thompson, 2011), or visibility (Gulati & Sanchez, 2002). In an examination of graduate students in psychology, attributes associated with superstar status were visibility, hard work, reflecting the graduate program's values, professor attachment, and an additional factor composed of characteristics related to being able to teach, not complaining, and accepting feedback well (Grover et al., 2006).

Superstars and great leaders are not necessarily the same people (Beggan, 2019b). One way to distinguish between a leader and a superstar concerns the way they make the trade-off between collective well-being and individual success. Leaders should be concerned with the welfare of their followers and the organization as a whole and not focus solely on their own accomplishments, whereas superstars are concerned for their own success. According to van Vugt and Ronay (2014, p. 86), "individual leaders competed with each other to attract followers but this competition was based more on prestige and respect than on dominance and coercion. This move away from dominance to prestige-based leadership was a pivotal step in human evolution."

One reason why great leaders can be hazardous is the tendency to confuse a great leader with a superstar. Achieving superstar status can make an individual sufficiently influential that he or she can move into a leadership role. It is also possible that success as a leader can give someone the status of a superstar. The question then becomes whether the superstar will work for his or her own welfare or for the welfare of the organization and its constituents.

Surprisingly, achieving superstar leader status may not benefit the leader or the organization he or she controls. The value placed on a superstar CEO can lead to a poor selection process (Khurana, 2002). Searches may be limited to current CEOs or presidents. Superstar CEOs may deliberately destabilize an organization (Khurana, 2002) in order to enact changes. Superstar CEOs, defined in terms of being award-winning, underperform relative to both their prior level of performance and similar other CEOs who have not won awards (Malmendier & Tate, 2009). Further, they extract more compensation in an absolute sense and relative to other high-ranking executives in the company.

In an analysis of bank recovery after the 2008 Great Recession, banks with narcissistic CEOs who operated in an environment of lax corporate governance (in the form of risk-taking) took longer to recover (Buyl, Boone, & Wade, 2019). The presence of a superstar CEO can reduce the quality of the strategic risk assessment from an outside auditor (Harvin & Killey, 2021). As noted by Malmendier and Tate (2009, p. 1634), "the celebrity culture permeating the business world has clear consequences for shareholders: increased status distorts CEO behavior and decreases subsequent firm performance." Regardless of how they finance their purchase, when CEOs buy extremely large or costly mansions or estates, the future performance of the company deteriorates, which suggests CEO entrenchment, i.e., a feeling of immunity from negative consequences of poor performance (Liu & Yermack, 2012).

The potential hazard associated with accepting the assumptions of superstardom is on display with the way that university presidents are hired, rewarded, fired, and in some cases rewarded as part of the termination process. Wilde and Finkelstein (2022, n.p.) noted, "Colleges can be on the hook for millions of dollars over the years for a presidential hire that didn't pan out. Now, however, we see a new group of failed presidents – those who resign amid allegations of various types of misdeeds but are still able to return to campus as senior-level, tenured faculty members." Finkelstein and Wilde (2017) described this process as the "CEO-ization" of the university presidency, which awarded exiting presidents with platinum parachutes. The potential cost of this investment does not include the expenses associated with hiring executive search firms to identify and interview candidates (Letiecq & Wilde, 2020), which can readily reach $300,000 and still fail to rule out problematic candidates.

We suspect that the hazard of great leadership is magnified when a leader takes on a title or an identity that is high in status. The more prestige associated with a professional title, the more hazardous is the leadership. "Pride goes before a fall." Holding a high-status position can be fraught with the danger of temptations that correspond to the potential influence of the seven deadly sins, a fact that could explain why university presidents, politicians, priests, and pastors are so often associated with scandals that destroy their reputations and end their careers. Psychologists have found that status has a corrupting influence on moral choices. Coughenour and her colleagues (2020), for example, found that drivers of new, expensive cars engage in ruder driving behaviors compared to drivers of older, cheaper cars.

Alternatively, according to the principles of *symbolic self-completion*, people use symbols as a means of self-definition (Wicklund & Gollwitzer, 2013). If those symbols are lacking or insufficient, people will compensate for perceived weaknesses by seeking out additional symbols of success along a relevant dimension (Wicklund & Gollwitzer, 1981). These strategies of compensation could involve purchasing or displaying artifacts associated with being successful or persuading others as to one's competency. In other words, a person who feels he or she lacks the evidence of being a great leader may become distracted from the actual work of leadership to take on symbolic representations of great leadership.

According to the processes of symbolic self-completion, a leader who suffers a setback or who feels he or she has attained enough, might be tempted to compensate in ways that are self-serving but could interfere with the smooth functioning of the organization. Paradoxically, the more successful leaders are, the more they might ultimately feel failure once their level of success plateaus.

3 Domains of Impact

A *toxic worker* engages in actions harmful to an organization or to people within that organization (Houseman & Minor, 2015). By extension, a *toxic leader* does so with a higher level of authority and status. Toxic leadership can manifest in a variety of forms (Saleem, Malik, & Malik, 2021), which include self-promotion, abusive supervision, narcissism, authoritarian leadership, and unpredictability. Unfortunately, a toxic leader can also be a high-performing person – a superstar – who may garner both formal and informal rewards and possess both formal and informal means of exercising power.

A leader can become a hazard in several domains. Perhaps most ironically, a great leader can undermine his or her own success and accomplishments by the very act of becoming an outstanding leader. A leader can also undermine followers. More broadly, a great leader can represent a threat to the organization in which he or she is employed. Finally, great leaders can become a danger to the larger society in which they and their organizations are embedded. The premise of this Element is that the negative consequences created by great leaders emerge from a variety of well-known social and psychological processes.

Threats to Leaders

Perhaps our most counterintuitive assertion is that a great leader can represent a hazard to himself or herself. Based on past success, great leaders may become overly enamored with their own abilities. Their pride gets in the way of their potential for success. Excessive optimism can result in a decrease in performance because people may prepare insufficiently (Brown & Marshall, 2001). Similarly, high self-esteem may interfere with performance, interpersonal success, happiness, and living a healthier lifestyle (Baumeister et al., 2003). *Hubris syndrome*, which develops after the acquisition of power, refers to a pattern of behavior marked by concern for self-image, which manifests as the desire for and the performance of behaviors that facilitate self-glorification (Owen & Jackson, 2009). Constituents, such as voters and shareholders, may be reluctant to criticize a leader who displays evidence of hubris syndrome because doing so would call into question their own judgment about supporting the person as a leader (Osnos, 2017). *Psychological entitlement* refers to an individual difference variable where someone feels he or she is owed special treatment without the need to reciprocate (Campbell et al., 2004; Naumann, Minsky, & Sturman, 2002). Leaders can develop a sense of entitlement, which can lead to them taking more for themselves (de Cremer & van Dijk, 2005).

Great leaders may set themselves up for future failure by expending less effort or being less concerned with the possible negative outcomes of failure, especially if they are insulated with generous severance packages (Cowen, King, & Marcel, 2016) or *mindguards*, i.e., people who shield them from disagreeable or contradictory information and analyses (Mulcahy, 1995). In other words, they may become victims of the sin of sloth. High-performing leaders may become addicted to power and deny their power addiction (Weidner & Purohit, 2009). Self-promoting CEOs may exaggerate their own successes (Malmendier & Tate, 2009). Pride and greed may undermine their potential for achievement.

Role conflicts between different aspects of being a leader can operate due to different demands that exist within the same job (Rizzo, House, & Lirtzman, 1970). For example, in the context of academic jobs, a leadership role, such as chair or dean, can interfere with other aspects of an academic appointment, specifically with regard to teaching or maintaining an active line of research. Another form of role conflict operates among different sectors of life, such as simultaneous demands between work and home life (Schueller-Weidekamm & Kautzky-Willer, 2012). The more accomplished a leader becomes, the more in demand he or she is likely to be, which will, in turn, create the potential for more stress.

In addition to potential conflict related to leaders performing their jobs, leaders are affected by personal problems and personal crises (Hickman & Knouse, 2020). Because of their importance to an organization, their hardships may have more far-reaching consequences for the organization itself as well as public beliefs about the organization. For example, even a false report that Steve Jobs of Apple had a heart attack was enough to play "havoc" with the stock price (Thomasch & Paul, 2008).

One trait that seems to have a complex relationship with leader success and the ability to achieve greatness involves the influence of charisma. Charismatic and noncharismatic leaders can be differentiated by personality traits involving an orientation toward cognitive achievement, enhanced creativity, risk-taking, but also a concern for a nonexploitive use of power (House & Howell, 1992). Overall, charismatic leaders encourage independence rather than subservience. There are two types of charismatic leadership (House & Howell, 1992). *Socialized* charismatic leadership involves egalitarian behavior that empowers, develops others, and is not motivated by the individual self-interests of the leader. With *personalized* charismatic leadership, influence is based on dominating, authoritarian behavior that exploits others and furthers the leader's own interests to the detriment of the organization as a whole.

As noted by Vergauwe et al. (2018, p. 125), "existing theories and research on leader charisma have in common that they all tend to depart from a rather simplistic 'more is better' perspective ... [with the] evidence increasing in favor of an alternative 'too much of a good thing' perspective in the fields of applied personality, organizational behavior, and management science." Our approach is consistent with a "too much of a good thing" perspective. In other words, charisma may influence leader effectiveness in a curvilinear fashion because of the inherent conflict between operational and strategic behavior (Vergauwe et al., 2018). *Strategic* behavior focuses on long-term goals, whereas *operational* behavior focuses on maintaining day-to-day operations of an organization or institution. Leaders low in charisma may fail because they lack strategic thinking. Leaders high in charisma may not succeed because they fail to focus on the small details involved in maintaining an organization. Further, at a high level, charisma can create a cult of personality (Strong & Killingsworth, 2011), where a self-defined savior presents himself or herself as an authentic and trustworthy representative of the people and opposed to traditional political elites (Wodak, 2017). As we will discuss in the section on the seven deadly sins, Donald Trump can be conceptualized as a leader working within the influence of a cult of personality (Reyes, 2020).

Groupthink refers to the way in which the desire for concurrence and the tendency to disregard risk can cause groups to adopt poor decision-making strategies, which, in turn, lead to poor decisions and outcomes (Goethals & Darley, 1987). The symptoms of groupthink include the illusion of invulnerability, collective rationalization, and self-censorship (Turner & Pratkanis, 1998). Other symptoms include the role of mindguards and an assumption of the inherent morality of the group. Followers may act as mindguards to make a leader feel accomplished in order to further their own ambitions. Thus, the seven deadly sins – such as pride and envy – as they appear in followers can subsequently have an indirect effect on leaders.

Because groups are more likely to experience groupthink when they operate under *directed leadership* (Turner & Pratkanis, 1998), it is possible to think of groupthink as a process that exists in the boundary between the leader and the follower. A strong leader – or someone who people believe to be a highly capable leader – may possess the kind of attributes or charisma that encourages groupthink; however, for groupthink to operate, the followers have to enable a leader by acting in a way to bias the leader toward a particular way of thinking. Although groupthink, as an explanatory concept, is not without its critics (Fuller & Aldag, 1998), factors used to understand groupthink can be applied to creating an environment where a leader's tendency to abuse the role may be encouraged.

Threats to Followers

Great leaders can harm followers in at least two ways. In a more corrupt form, when a great leader abuses the role, he or she can do damage to a follower. Alternatively, even a well-intentioned leader can take advantage of a follower through variables such as a follower's trust in a leader or role-based status and power differences. In the context of leadership, we suggest that great leaders encourage great loyalty, which can be abused if followers are compelled to choose between engaging in an ethical action and remaining loyal to a leader (Zhang et al., 2020). Although whistleblowers can be viewed as acting in accord with a higher principle (Black, 2016), they are often stigmatized as being disloyal to their own organization or the leadership structure of that organization (Grant, 2002).

Loyalty to a leader can cause a follower to take risks or engage in actions that protect a leader or facilitate a leader's goals, even when doing so is objectively not the correct strategy. With *misguided* loyalty, a follower initiates a course of action that would ultimately prove ill-advised. With *mistaken* loyalty, a leader takes advantage of a follower by asking him or her to do something that is potentially illegal or unethical. Loyal followers may not necessarily be motivated by positive values. They may help even a corrupt leader to further their own ends. This dynamic can produce a vicious cycle of the operation of the seven deadly sins. A leader may put his or her own needs ahead of others' due to motivations such as greed, pride, wrath, or envy. In turn, greedy or ambitious followers may feed the leader's desires as a means of enhancing their own status – even if it means the destruction of the leader or the organization in the process.

Two kinds of followers are susceptible to leaders' ambitions. A *colluder* has similar ambitions and goals as the leader and conforms with or enables a leader's desires as a means of achieving personal success. A *conformer* goes along with the status quo to maintain his or her own position or job but not to advance personal, perhaps selfish or toxic, agendas.

Even a great leader may inadvertently take advantage of a follower because of social-psychological principles associated with leader and follower roles. Possessing power can reduce an individual's ability to take on another's perspective (Galinsky et al., 2006). As such, leaders can lose empathy for and become less able to identify with followers. Leaders can become isolated for a number of reasons, including the desire for safety, because they believe they are entitled to preferential treatment or because at least some constituents attempt to isolate them from others.

Power may reduce perspective-taking for several reasons. First, people in power control resources. As such, they may be less dependent on others to facilitate their own goals. Additionally, people in power tend to be the center of attention and have demands placed on their time and attention. As a result, they may have fewer cognitive resources to attend to the needs or feelings of others; if they are high in dominance, they may not even have the desire to do so (Fiske, 1993).

Although a harsh leadership style such as displays of anger (Koning & Van Kleef, 2015) can reduce follower motivation (Yip & Walker, 2022), paradoxically a highly successful leader can also decrease follower motivation. This reduction in motivation can occur if followers develop less interest in the organization and show less initiative in working or solving problems because they believe their leader will do the work for them. One consequence of reduced motivation is that followers may show less creativity with their work duties. Further, they may develop less felt responsibility for the organization or their own obligations if they believe their contribution will be outweighed by the work of a leader. A leader's success can also increase follower resentment because followers can become envious of a leader's benefits, such as enhanced status and salary.

Threats to the Organization

Leaders can harm their organizations when their goals conflict with organizational goals. Because there may be few checks on a leader's behavior, leaders may have little accountability to an organization. As a result, a leader's personal scandals can hurt an organization's reputation. Perhaps the clearest example of this process involved the consequences of sexual harassment in the workplace, which led to the growth of the #MeToo movement (Beggan, 2019b).

Leaders can also delay organizational change. *Founder's syndrome* is a situation where a person possesses special privileges and exerts influential power over the company or institution he or she started (Block & Rosenberg, 2002). This social influence can also operate through the perceptions of others, such as employees, members of the media, or the public. An implication of the term "syndrome" is that, after a certain point, the influence of the founder may become destructive to the overall well-being of the company, which can lead to the failure of the organization (Block, 2004).

A highly competent leader can impair organizational efficiency by fostering social loafing (Karau & Williams, 1993), which can be defined as "decreases in individual motivation when working on group or collective tasks" (Karau, 2020, p. xii). One factor that can mitigate the operation of social loafing in the workplace is if a leader adopts a strategy of servant leadership (Stouten & Liden, 2020). Servant leadership operates as a form of humility that can counteract the deadly sin of pride. According to Greenleaf (1977, p. 27, emphasis in original):

> The servant-leader *is* servant first ... It begins with the natural feeling that one wants to serve, to serve *first*. Then conscious choice brings one to aspire to lead ... The best test, and difficult to administer, is this: Do those served grow as persons? Do they, *while being served*, become healthier, wiser, freer, more autonomous, and more likely themselves to become servants? *And*, what is the effect on the least privileged in society? Will they benefit, or at least not further be deprived?

Threats to Society

Leaders who become so focused on their own outcomes – either personal or in terms of the organization – may make choices that have detrimental effects on the larger society in which they and their organization exist. These processes can operate within legal boundaries. For example, a number of industries have been slow to acknowledge the negative effects of global warming (Eavis & Krauss, 2021); however, doing so is not a crime. In other instances, however, a leader's behavior can cross into actual criminal activity. For example, Donald Trump has succeeded in radicalizing the Republican Party (Lurie, 2021), which is not in itself a crime. However, his actions may become criminal if, for example, it is determined that he conspired to overturn an election, as proposed by the January 6 insurrection committee (Baker & Benner, 2022).

Because the dominant cultural conceptualization of great leaders is that they are older, white, and male (Eagley & Chin, 2010; Koenig et al., 2011; Rudic, Hubner, & Baum, 2021), from an intersectionality perspective, non-majority individuals tend to face additional challenges in their efforts to attain leadership roles or perform as leaders (Sanchez-Hucles & Davis, 2010). As such, great leaders who conform to the stereotypic representation – merely because their success reinforces that representation – interfere with other potential leaders establishing themselves if they do not conform to that representation.

4 The Seven Deadly (and Hazardous) Sins of Great Leadership

With the statement "Great men are almost always bad men," Lord Acton (1949) appears to turn the world upside-down, with our heroes operating in disguise as villains and vice versa. His assertion is jarring. Can it possibly be true? And can we, by extension, infer that great *leaders* are almost always bad men? Were he alive today, Acton might qualify the statement to read that great people can easily become villains, or are a bit more prone to sliding into villainy, as compared to ordinary people. In the Bible, Jesus makes the similar claim about "how hard it is for the rich to enter the kingdom of God" (Mark 10:23). There are in fact several scriptural references to the dangers of worshiping money or hoarding an excess of riches. Buddhist texts warn of the dangers of attachment to power and money. Letting go of the illusion of having power and no longer identifying oneself with power hold the key to achieving freedom from suffering (Brown, 2022).

All humans are vulnerable to falling prey to the seven deadly sins, yet Lord Acton somehow intuited that great people are especially vulnerable. Why might greatness in a person place them at greater risk of sinning to a deadly degree? In the early nineteenth century, Lord Acton's knowledge of the history of

European tyrants and monarchs prompted him to conclude that power, fame, and wealth all conspire to bring out the worst in people. Scholars in the twenty-first century now have at their disposal scientific methods that provide compelling evidence that power corrupts both the brain and behavior.

One of the splash headlines of 2017 was "Power Causes Brain Damage," which was the eye-catching title of an article in *The Atlantic*, authored by Jerry Useem. This publication not only brought attention to the ways that power compromises one's morality; it also illuminated Dacher Keltner's (2016) social-psychological research on how power debilitates the mind in ways that mirror damage done by traumatic brain injury.

Earlier we noted Coughenour and colleagues' (2020) and Galinsky and colleagues' (2006) research showing that power can reduce taking other people's perspectives into account. More generally, giving ordinary people the feeling of power tends to swell the ego, deflate empathy, increase a sense of entitlement, and decrease one's tendency to behave in a prosocial manner. In other words, a taste of power can encourage the influence of the seven deadly sins. These studies seem to bear out a great deal of what Sigmund Freud (1922) wrote about group leaders sharing similarities with the chiefs of the "primal horde." Their sexuality was uninhibited, they had little care for others except if they were useful, and they were highly narcissistic and primed to act. Specifically, the leader "loved no one but himself, or other people only so far as they served his needs ... he may be of a masterful nature, absolutely narcissistic, self-confident and independent" (p. 71).

Magee et al. (2005) showed, for example, that people who feel powerful have a strong action orientation. In one study when participants were in a room with an annoying fan blowing on them, those feeling powerful were more likely to move the fan or turn it off. They are also less inhibited. If sitting in a room with another person and a plate of sweets, they were more likely to take the last cookie and more likely to leave crumbs on the table. Both men and women who felt powerful were more likely to flirt. Of special importance are studies showing their disregard for others. They acted from their own perspective rather than other people's, exaggerated their own contributions to group tasks, diminished those of others, and generally showed less interest in meeting or interacting with others. Other people were to be used, if acknowledged at all.

Despite all these cautions about the dangers of wielding power and hoarding money, when people are asked to list their heroes the names of super-wealthy individuals invariably appear on their lists: Bill Gates, Kim Kardashian, Tom Brady, Alice Walton, and Tiger Woods are all striking examples of people's heroes (Allison & Goethals, 2011). Rightly or wrongly, our society tends to equate wealth with greatness.

Many of our wealthiest and most admired celebrities took a great fall during the #MeToo movement that began in 2006 but gained momentum in 2017 (Beggan, 2019b; Nicolaou & Smith, 2019). Great people who fulfilled Lord Acton's prophecy of becoming bad people include Bill Cosby, Matt Lauer, Kevin Spacey, Harvey Weinstein, and Louis C. K. These individuals' actions were not just disturbing; they were also surprising given that the perpetrators were self-professed progressives who presented themselves as highly civilized and enlightened. Every day, news headlines – whether they involve the Catholic Church, the Boy Scouts, or women's athletic teams' doctors and coaches – would appear to confirm Lord Acton's dictum about power turning people who *should* be great into people who belong in prison.

We briefly review each of the seven deadly sins in what follows, discussing each sin in comparison to its opposing virtue. We discuss sloth, gluttony, and lust together. Pride is cured by the virtue of humility; envy by kindness; wrath by meekness; sloth by diligence; greed by charity; gluttony by temperance; and lust by chastity. We suggest that the seven deadly sins can help explain why great leaders may become hazardous. They succumb to the temptations associated with the seven deadly sins, put their own outcomes ahead of their followers or the organization, and end up as liabilities rather than assets.

Pride and Its Antidote, Humility

Power appears to inflate one's pride – the first and most destructive of the seven deadly sins. Dante Alighieri's (1320/2009) definition of pride, as described in *The Divine Comedy*, was "love of self perverted to hatred and contempt for one's neighbor" (canto 10, line 130). Pride is so central to the seven deadly sins that it is seen as the driving force behind all the remaining sins. The tendency to be proud of oneself, and to take mental and behavioral steps to self-enhance, is considered by psychologists to be the most central mechanism governing our sense of self (Sedikides & Strube, 1997). Destructive traits related to pride include hubris, narcissism, ambition, arrogance, and overconfidence.

There are many examples of leadership gone awry because of excessive pride, self-esteem, and overconfidence. In Greek mythology, the excessive pride of Oedipus, the king of Thebes, convinced him that he could escape the unavoidable fate of marrying his mother and murdering his father. Icarus sought to reach the sun with wings made of wax and feathers. His hubris blinded him to the reality of the sun melting the wax and hurling him back down to earth. Shakespearean tragic heroes such as King Lear and Macbeth shared the flaw of inflated ego, and the results were disastrous for them and for their societies. Macbeth's sense of entitlement sends him on a murder spree, and Lear's excessive pride leads to estrangement from his daughters and the collapse of his kingdom.

Real-world leaders are no less immune to pride's deadly consequences. Many advanced civilizations – ancient Egypt and Rome, and Nazi Germany, to name only three – have collapsed due to reckless overconfidence and overexuberant nationalism. Sadly, there is no shortage of modern-day nations who are led by prideful, narcissistic leaders. Consider Vladimir Putin's self-destructive warrior tendencies, Donald Trump's unwillingness to concede election defeat, and Kim Jong-un's desperate need for worldwide military attention. Some have called these men living embodiments of toxic masculinity (Harrington, 2021). The lesson from history is clear: Individuals and nations with power, or who harbor a need to accumulate power, will often self-destruct. Even worse, their own self-destruction heaps vast collateral damage on millions of innocents.

Two of the authors of this Element reside in central Virginia, which in 2011 sustained an earthquake with a magnitude of 5.8 on the Richter scale. Located just a few miles from the epicenter of the quake was the North Anna nuclear power plant. Built in 1980, it was designed to withstand a quake as large as 6.0. This extremely narrow margin of error demonstrates how overconfident leaders are, even in situations where overconfidence could cost the lives of millions of people. No one in Virginia was killed, but the same cannot be said for the citizens of New Orleans in 2005 when Hurricane Katrina devastated much of the city. Despite its location on the vulnerable coast of the Gulf of Mexico, and despite being below sea level, New Orleans was ill-prepared for a major hurricane. City leaders deemed the levees protecting the city to be sufficient, and more than a thousand human beings perished because of this tragic overconfidence.

Pride can be viewed as an excessive appreciation of one's own accomplishments. The myth of Narcissus involves a man who falls in love with his own image and stares at it until he dies. Another way to think about pride as it operates with the leader–follower relationship is that followers can be a reflective surface that feeds back the self-focused attention the leader desires.

The antidote to pride is the virtue of humility. Just as pride is viewed as the most destructive of all the sins, philosophers and ethicists view humility as the greatest of all virtues (Worthington, Davis, & Hook, 2017). Humility can be broken down into three components. Humble leaders (1) have an accurate sense of themselves, i.e., are aware of their limitations and are therefore teachable; (2) show sincere modesty; and (3) are oriented to advancing others. Humble leaders have power but use their power not for self-aggrandizement but to build others up rather than squash them down.

Humble leaders listen to feedback and make appropriate adjustments to their behavior when necessary. They are open-minded, accountable, and willing to admit their mistakes. They not only accept critical feedback; they encourage it. Humble leaders help others and ask for help when they need it. They treat others with respect and do not hesitate to credit others, acknowledging the reality that collective success is a team effort rather than a simple reflection of leadership effectiveness.

Perhaps the most important "takeaway" from this section on the deadly sin of pride is *not* that having high self-esteem is bad and that holding a positive self-image is wrong. Successful leaders should act with confidence and decisiveness. The more our actions reveal the courage of our convictions, the more we will inspire others and accomplish our group's goals. *The takeaway is that leaders should seek a balance between pride and humility.* The idea of "finding a balance" is probably an overused expression these days, but leaders who fail to achieve an equilibrium here run the risk of either acting like a narcissistic bully or becoming a soft, rudderless doormat.

Often, we can turn to fictional storytelling to guide us in matters of finding a healthy balance between two extremes. In the original *Star Trek* television series, there is an episode called "The Enemy Within," in which Captain James T. Kirk beams up from a planet's surface during a bad storm. The ship's transporter malfunctions and literally splits Kirk into two different people, each of whom looks exactly like Kirk. One Kirk possesses his aggressive and prideful lust for power. The other Kirk, in contrast, is gentle, humble, and meek. At first, everyone on the ship believes that the softer Kirk is the real Kirk and that the dark, narcissistic Kirk is an imposter. However, Kirk's first officer Mr. Spock is able to recognize that both Kirks are equally essential for making Kirk's great leadership possible. The crew fixes the transporter and merges the two Kirks together, once again forming a balanced leader.

We mention this episode of *Star Trek* for two reasons. First and most obviously, we wish to underscore a caveat to Lord Acton's declaration that all great men are bad men. Captain Kirk's dark, prideful side was not a bad quality, because it was kept in check by his kinder, gentler side. Kirk's greatness was derived from his ability to find the sweet spot between these two extremes. The second reason we mention *Star Trek* is that it becomes very clear that Kirk's great leadership does not happen in a social vacuum. To operate as an effective and balanced leader, Kirk seeks input from trusted colleagues. The triumvirate of Kirk, Spock, and Dr. McCoy is a balanced and harmonious blending of the archetypes of physicality, reason, and emotion. Captain Kirk owes much of his success to his ability and willingness to seek advice from Spock, who is the consummate logician, and from McCoy, who has emotional wisdom. Kirk keeps his prideful side in check by consulting with his friends and receiving accurate and sometimes humbling feedback from them.

Pride, we argue, is not a deadly sin when its possessor takes steps to balance it with the humble practices of listening to others, keeping an open mind, and acknowledging and correcting mistakes. The ancient Roman philosopher Marcus Tullius Cicero once wisely said, "The higher we are placed, the more humbly we should walk."

Envy and Its Antidote, Kindness

Another hazard of great leadership is the experience of envy. *Envy* is defined as wanting something that someone else has. Dante (Alighieri 1320/2009) described envy as the "love of one's own good perverted to a desire to deprive other men of theirs" (canto 13, line 78). Envy is so destructive that it is the one deadly sin that appears in the Ten Commandments: "Thou shalt not covet thy neighbor's goods." Emotions that accompany envy include a longing for things that one is lacking mixed with anger or resentment toward people who have those things. Envy is often confused with jealousy, but these two emotions are distinct (Parrott & Smith, 1993). Envy is the desire for something that is possessed by someone else, whereas *jealousy* is a fear that someone will take from you something that is already in your possession. A husband becomes jealous if his wife flirts with another man because he fears his wife will leave him for his rival. A husband will be envious of another man if that man has a better sense of humor. He wishes he had that same attribute. Envy can create jealousy if a husband worries that his rival's better sense of humor will lure his wife away.

Envy is one of the seven deadly sins because it divides people. It ruins relationships, propagates discord, and engenders bitterness and spite. Envy brings out the worst in people, inspiring them to act and speak in toxic ways. Envious people are unlikely to live in harmony with each other. The emotion provokes hostility, resentment, anger, and irritability. Envy cultivates a victim mentality – a focus on the good things that are lacking rather than on the good things that are already in one's possession. Psychologists have found that obsessive envy is associated with depression, anxiety, and prejudice (Wu et al., 2020).

The story of Cain and Abel in Genesis 4 of the Old Testament is a striking and archetypal illustration of the destructive effects of envy. Both brothers made a sacrifice to please God, but God only acknowledged Abel's gift, not Cain's. Here, it is important to remember that all seven deadly sins, including envy, stem from the primary sin of pride. Because of his pride, Cain saw himself as blameless and incorrectly identified Abel as the cause of this problem. Cain's inability, or unwillingness, to acknowledge the inadequacy of his own gift to God prompted him to kill his brother Abel. Envy has the power to kill relationships. As Lord Acton admonished, this kind of power can corrupt us all, resulting in disaster for leaders themselves as well as for others.

Leadership effectiveness can be compromised by envy. Several US presidents showed an unhealthy envy for their predecessors, often at the nation's expense. In his biography of President Lyndon B. Johnson, Peters (2010, p. 98) describes Johnson's envy of John F. Kennedy's youth, good looks, charisma, and popularity. Johnson resented the Kennedy family's much-ballyhooed social sophistication, boasting that his Texan ancestors were intellectuals and college presidents "when the Kennedys in this country were still tending bar." After Kennedy was assassinated in 1963, Johnson was irritated by the public's adoration of Kennedy and pernicious rumors that Johnson had engineered the assassination.

Peters (2010) argues that Johnson's 1964 launching of his war on poverty, civil rights legislation, and Vietnam conflict escalation all reflected a drive to surpass the Kennedy legacy. Driven by envy and competitive motives, Johnson felt he had to push through initiatives that were more impactful than what Kennedy would have achieved. Legislation to combat poverty and systemic racism were noble, of course. However, Johnson's steadfast commitment to winning an unwinnable war in Vietnam was fueled by his relentless competition with the ghost of Kennedy. Envy, then, may have contributed to the deaths of tens of thousands of Americans and Vietnamese.

Another powerful example of the destructive effects of envy is the obsessive resentment that former President Donald Trump had for his predecessor in the White House, former President Barack Obama. Authors and journalists have documented this extreme envy-driven animus (e.g., Bostock, 2020; Chait, 2021; Ewers, 2020; Robinson, 2019; Smith, 2020). Before becoming president, Trump led the "birther" conspiracy, arguing that Obama was not born in America. These claims persisted even after Obama produced a legal and legitimate birth certificate proving his birth in Hawaii. Trump may have had racist motives here, but scholars have argued that Trump was also highly envious of the public's admiration for Obama (Moore, 2018).

Shortly after his inauguration, Trump falsely claimed that his inauguration attendance exceeded that of Obama. Later during his term as president, Trump declared that his economy was better than Obama's and that his popularity was greater. Both these claims were refuted by fact-checkers (Farley & Robertson, 2017). Throughout his term as president, Trump tried to erase Obama's legacy, reversing many of Obama's executive orders and legislative victories. Trump undid many of Obama's greenhouse gas regulations and pulled the United States out of the Paris Climate Agreement. Although Trump tried to repeal the Affordable Healthcare Act, he was unsuccessful because he underestimated public support for Obama's healthcare reform.

Michael Cohen, Donald Trump's former lawyer and consultant, has said that Trump's hatred of Obama derived from envy. In an interview with MSNBC's Rachel Maddow, Cohen explained what it was about Obama that Trump coveted: "He's Black. He went to Harvard Law. He graduated at the top of his class. He's incredibly articulate," Cohen said. "He is all the things that Donald Trump wants to be, and he just can't handle it," Cohen added. "And what do you do if you can't handle it, and you're Donald Trump? You attack it" (Bostock, 2020, p. 1). One way of attacking Obama was through Twitter. Between November 2010 and May 2020, Trump tweeted about Obama 2,933 times, and none of these tweets was flattering (Smith, 2020). This startling number means that Trump, on average, composed nearly one disparaging tweet about Obama per day for almost ten years. Trump is the poster child of obsessive envy and resentment.

Although we have focused on how a leader's experience of envy can negatively influence his or her effectiveness, envy may be an emotion that is especially influential with followers who wish to have the success they see in a leader. They want what the leader has. As such, they may display the same ultimately destructive behaviors as a leader to get the rewards the leader has. They may facilitate a leader's ambitions as a means to satisfy their own. Of course, to the extent that a leader is overcompensated – such as in the case of CEO compensation – the lure of the leader as a target of envy increases.

How does one overcome feelings of envy? Juliana Brienes (2013) suggests several science-based remedies. She recommends first acknowledging envy as reflecting an all-too human insecurity and dissatisfaction with oneself. Recognizing and admitting our feelings of envy can be followed by showing self-compassion. To feel occasional envy is to be human. Next, almost counterintuitively, we can show compassion for the target of our envy. Brienes makes the point that the people we envy are struggling in ways that are invisible to us. She also suggests using our envy as fuel for self-improvement. Although Sedikides and Strube (1997) identified prideful self-serving tendencies as the primary self-process, they also identified the drive for self-improvement as a secondary core self-process that can mitigate the destructive effects of selfish envy. Brienes also suggests the practice of gratitude as an effective antidote. Focusing on what one has been given, rather than on one's deficits, has been shown to increase self-esteem and overall well-being (Wood, Froh, & Geraghty, 2010).

Wrath and Its Antidote, Meekness

Dante's (Alighieri 1320/2009) description of wrath was "love of justice perverted to revenge and spite" (canto 8, line 126). Wrath, put simply, is an intense emotional anger. As the great orator Robert G. Ingersoll (1915, p. 74) once said,

"Anger is the wind that blows out the light of reason." Leaders who aspire to greatness cannot afford to allow anger to rob them of their sound judgment.

Psychologists have identified four variations of anger, some of which are more destructive than others to good leadership (Ni, 2014). The first type of anger is rarely seen among adults but is very real to anyone who has parented a child. This is the *temper tantrum*, defined as an unreasonable and disproportionate outburst. Tantrums are a normal part of development, and although most people outgrow them, some adult narcissists continue to show such outbursts when they do not get their way. Usually such individuals are unable to enjoy healthy relationships and thus rarely reach positions of responsible leadership. The second type, *annoyance anger*, is defined as the feeling of irritation that occurs when we encounter bad drivers, rude store clerks, or a splinter in our finger. Annoyances are normal and rarely affect leadership ability.

The third kind of anger, however, has the potential to turn great leaders into disastrous leaders. *Aggressive* anger causes people to dominate, intimidate, and control others. When people show aggressive anger, they can easily morph into bullies, oppressors, and abusers. A toxic personality trait associated with aggressive anger is the *authoritarian personality* (Adorno et al., 1950), which is characterized by rigid, destructive perceptions of the social world and by the need to control and manipulate others for self-gain. Authoritarians are often deeply insecure individuals who mask their fragile self-esteem with self-enhancing lies and displays of anger and dominance over others.

Authoritarian personalities project their sense of inferiority onto other people in the form of harsh negative evaluations of rivals, racial groups, and other nations. Leaders who show authoritarian tendencies tend to judge others in black-and-white terms, as winners and losers, as "us" versus "them." Authoritarians have a cynical view of humanity, a fear of outsiders, a need to wield power and show toughness, an anti-intellectual view of the world, and an exaggerated concern with sexual perversion. Ron Riggio (2009) describes how authoritarians, as bad leaders, often resort to "cheap psychological tricks" to attract support from followers. These tricks include creating in-group and out-group factions, using threats and punishments, and demanding obedience to authority.

A textbook example of the authoritarian personality is former President Donald Trump (Neiwert, 2018). Raised by a father who brutalized him, Trump attended a military school that instilled in him "a blueprint for leadership by force and ridicule" (Taddonio, 2020, p. 1). He ruled his school dormitory with an iron fist, separating classmates into "winners" and "losers." Trump the presidential candidate in 2016 made a habit of boasting about factually incorrect self-attributes. Before being elected, he proclaimed himself, "the healthiest individual ever elected to the presidency," despite clear evidence that he was overweight (Taylor, 2018). Trump called Mexican immigrants "rapists" and derogated women with such labels as "horseface," "dogs," "fat pigs," and "nasty." Trump the authoritarian attracted authoritarian followers. In his doctoral dissertation, Matthew McWilliams (2016) found that the number-one predictor of whether a voter supported Trump was the voter's authoritarian personality tendencies, a far better predictor of support for Trump than voters' age, race, income, or education level.

Trump not only attracted authoritarian followers; he turned nonauthoritarian followers into authoritarians (Merryman, 2018). Social scientists have found that bad behaviors – especially bad behaviors shown by leaders – are contagious. Anger, blaming, bullying, and incivility are all *social contagions* and can mutate into social super-viruses. Fast and Tiedens (2010) found that after people read about their governor blaming others for his failures, they were more likely themselves to blame others for their own personal failures. Twenge and Campbell's (2010) research shows that when leaders brag about their superiority and accomplishments, it normalizes narcissism among their followers. Research also shows that people are more likely to lie and cheat after they have seen someone get away with lying and cheating (Gino, Ayal, & Ariely, 2009).

Alarmingly, social scientists have found that bad behavior is more impactful and infectious than good behavior (Baumeister et al., 2001). Studies of social media have shown that anger travels faster than joy (Anderson et al., 2018). Porath and Erez (2007) found that exposure to just a mild dose of incivility undermines one's willingness to be courteous as well as one's ability to show creativity in problem-solving. Things are even worse when leaders, or role models, show bad behavior. About 25 percent of the most uncivil employees act that way because their boss is uncivil (Schilpzand, De Pater, & Erez, 2016). Authoritarian leadership, and the inevitable anger that goes with it, spreads to followers like an infectious disease. Research has shown, for example, that Trump's incivility on social media engendered a normalization of bad behavior from his followers (Knobe, 2017). It appears that Lord Acton's dictum about great men also being bad men does not go far enough. Great men who become bad men also turn other great men into bad men.

The good news is that positive behaviors are also contagious. Studies show that being on the receiving end of generosity makes you more likely to be generous (Tsvetkov & Macy, 2014). Posting civil comments on social media can inspire others to post civil comments (Anderson et al., 2018). Organizations with enforced civility policies do better than organizations lacking such policies (Porath & Gerbasi, 2015).

For a leader to resist becoming a hazard through the operation of wrath, it is imperative that they maintain civil discourse, knowing that both good and bad behavior has the power to have a ripple effect on social and political well-being. Because bad behavior has more psychological impact and spreads faster than good behavior, leaders must be especially vigilant in avoiding any display of temper and incivility. In the heat of the moment, it is better to do and say nothing than to infect the world with emotional toxins. Best of all, leaders would be wise to follow Michelle Obama's (2016) suggestion, at the 2016 Democratic National Convention, to counter incivility with civility: "When they go low, we go high." Explaining what she meant, Obama emphasized the importance of flipping the negativity script and becoming a positive role model for the next generation.

The fourth type of anger is called *justifiable anger*. The key to understanding this type of anger is that any kind of justification is a mental construction, prone to distortion. Most people have no trouble justifying their wrath. Justifiable anger is described as the moral outrage we feel at the terrible injustices directed at us or at the world. At the personal level, we can be angry with romantic partners who hurt us, bosses who mistreat us, or the world in general for not giving us what we think we are entitled to. At the global level, we can be justifiably angry at the destruction of the environment, cruelty toward animals, or human rights abuses.

Justifiable anger may have some benefits, such as mobilizing us for action and for change. However, any type of anger over time is inherently unhealthy, robs us of peace of mind, and causes suffering. Buddhism teaches its practitioners that anger is the worst emotion and should be nipped in the bud as soon as it arises. From the Buddhist perspective, there is no anger that can be justified. To quell anger impulses, Buddhists use tools such as patience, detachment, meditation, empathy, gratitude, and humility. The goal is to let go of anger, and to let go of the illusion that anger can be justified, before it causes any suffering to oneself or others.

Recovery programs such as Alcoholics Anonymous (AA) also emphasize the folly of trying to justify anger. The founder of AA, Bill Wilson (1953, p. 90), pondered the question of justifiable anger. "If somebody cheats us, aren't we entitled to be mad? Can't we be properly angry with self-righteous folk? For us of AA, these are dangerous exceptions." Wilson believed that alcoholics are not "skillful in separating justified from unjustified anger. As we saw it, our wrath was always justified. Anger, that occasional luxury of more balanced people, could keep us on an emotional jag indefinitely." Wilson's conclusion about the temptation to justify anger is definitive: "*We have found that justified anger ought to be left to those better qualified to handle it*" (emphasis added).

Lord Acton might argue that no one, not even a person who is not an alcoholic, is qualified to handle anger. This is especially true for "great men" whose pride and anger can transform them into "bad men." When we are angry, we are almost always outwardly focused on what we believe is the cause of our anger. Other people are usually deemed the causal agent. Thus, to ameliorate anger, most of the world's spiritual traditions prescribe an inward focus rather than an outward focus. As Bill Wilson (1953, p. 90, emphasis in original) explains, "It is a spiritual axiom that every time we are disturbed, no matter what the cause, there is something wrong *with us.*" Another member of AA writes, "people and circumstances don't make us angry; *we* make ourselves angry. People *can't* make us angry – unless we let them. We alone are responsible for our feelings" (O., 1999, p. 43, emphasis in original).

Greed and Its Antidote, Charity

Dante (Alighieri 1320/2009) described greed as "excessive love of money and power" (canto 6, line 75). Human beings, and Americans especially, have always had a complicated relationship with greed. Sure, it is one of the seven deadly sins, and yes, most spiritual traditions, including the Bible, caution against the boundless love of wealth (e.g., Ecclesiastes 5:10 and 1 Timothy 6:10). And yet, there is no denying the love affair people have for money, billionaires, and ultrasuccessful businessmen and businesswomen. The appeal of greed was well represented in the 1987 movie *Wall Street*, starring Michael Douglas, who played the character of Wall Street magnate Gordon Gekko. Gekko uttered the iconic line from the film that most attracted the attention of moviegoers: "*Greed, for lack of a better word, is good. Greed is right. Greed works.*"

Throughout the movie, Gekko becomes increasingly unscrupulous and unsavory, ending up in jail. Although it should be obvious that he is the story's villain, audiences resonated with his charisma, good looks, and relentless pursuit of wealth-building and upward mobility. In the minds of the moviegoing public, Gekko was a hero, albeit a flawed hero, and his flaw resided not in his misbehavior but in being caught misbehaving. The movie inspired a new generation of stockbrokers and only reinforced America's worship of the kind of unbridled avarice that gave rise to dozens of financial scandals in the early twenty-first century.

Greed continues to be a venerated trait today. The world's richest 1 percent now owns half of the world's wealth (Lyons, 2017). The CEO of Legacy Advisory Partners, David Harper, consults with business leaders about the cautionary tales of criminal greed shown by Enron, Tyco, Lehman Brothers, Bear Sterns, and Bernie Madoff. "These are just a few high-profile examples of how unfettered greed can take down an organization and upend the lives of many innocent people," wrote Harper (2017, p. 1). The author Richard Eskow (2013, p. 1) said, "Love of money for money's sake is the social disease of our time." The psychologist and philosopher Erich Fromm (1992, p. 60) spent his career examining different destructive types of human character. He came to believe that "Greed is a bottomless pit which exhausts the person in an endless effort to satisfy the need without ever reaching satisfaction."

Perhaps the source of our ambivalence toward greed resides in its similarity to the mostly positive traits of ambition, passion, drive, vision, and achievement orientation. Do we conflate greed with an enterprising spirit? To be successful may require a pinch or more of greed, making greed similar to pride in that some small amount of these sins is necessary to fuel good healthy growth.

Once again, we are confronted with the likelihood that a fine line exists between sin and virtue and between hero and villain. A fascinating case study is Greg Norman, a former professional golf champion who had dashing good looks, great success in golf, and impressive triumphs in many business ventures. Norman has spent his life straddling the line between hero and villain, and both the public and his golfing peers are polarized in their opinions of him. Some view him as a greedy narcissist, whereas others see him as an accomplished visionary maverick (Associated Press, 2022).

Norman's latest business venture has sparked enormous controversy in the world of professional golf. In 2021, funded by the deep pockets of the Saudi Arabian government, Norman announced that he was establishing a new professional golf tour called the LIV Golf Invitational Tour. Over the next twelve months, Norman was able to lure many major star players from the PGA Tour to the LIV Golf Tour by promising them guaranteed money, in some cases hundreds of millions of dollars per player. Historically, pro golfers have had to earn their paychecks. Thus, LIV Golf's huge guaranteed payouts represented a seismic departure from the old business model. Norman sowed deep divisions in professional golf. There is now considerable acrimony between players remaining loyal to the old PGA Tour and those defecting to the new and more lucrative LIV Golf Tour.

Criticisms of Greg Norman's LIV Golf, which focused on four points relating to greed, concern the hazard posed by superstars. First, the sheer size of player salaries far exceeds the level of earnings players previously received under the business model of the PGA Tour. Second, LIV golfers are not earning these unprecedented sums of money; they are guaranteed this money. Third, and perhaps more importantly, is the source of the payouts to LIV golfers – the Saudi Arabian government. Critics have pointed to the Saudis' involvement in the terrorist attacks on September 11, 2001, the government's long history of civil rights abuses, the Saudi leader's 2018 assassination of *Washington Post* journalist Jamal Khashoggi, and the overall ruthless, totalitarian nature of the government. To receive LIV Golf's money is to be given "blood money." The fourth criticism of Greg Norman and LIV Golf centers on the new tour's emphasis on making the richest pro golfers even richer. To give his new tour legitimacy, Norman recruited many of the best and most successful players from the PGA Tour and other world tours. Thanks to LIV Golf, the gap between the best-paid and lowest-paid pro golfers, which was already considerable, has now become a wide chasm.

Is LIV Golf an example of greed run amok or a smart, new, visionary business model? Golfers and fans are split on this issue. There are outcries of greed and arrogance (Associated Press, 2022), but there are also expressions of admiration for Norman's leadership. Criticisms of Norman often center on his past reputation as a narcissist. During his long career as a player and businessman, Norman has been described as surly, standoffish, and self-centered (Ritz, 2022). Moreover, some of his top players on the LIV Golf Tour, such as Phil Mickelson and Patrick Reed, have also been singled out for their greed and narcissism. Early in his golf career, Mickelson was known by fellow players as FIG-JAM: "Fuck I'm Great – Just Ask Me" (Kelley, 2019). Reed has been described as cocky, friendless, and prone to cheating in golf (Notelovitz, 2021). Norman, Mickelson, and Reed may demonstrate how sinful traits such as pride and greed may interact or combine in ways that accentuate bad behavior.

The jury is out on the question of whether Greg Norman's LIV Golf Tour has a future in the sport. If Norman's new tour fizzles out, his greed and over-exuberant need for power and influence will be seen as contributing to his demise. If his new tour succeeds, Norman may be revered as a pioneer who revolutionized golf. Once again, we are reminded of Lord Acton's caution about the slippery slope from greatness to badness. Succumbing to the seven deadly sins may be the dark conduit from potential hero to potential villain. Only time will tell if Norman has overstepped the bounds of decency.

Greed and envy may operate together in both leaders and followers to intensify the potential that a great leader has in becoming a hazard. A great leader may want more and resent other leaders who are more successful. Followers may emulate both a great leader and a corrupt great leader as a means of getting what those leaders possess. Their greed and envy motivate them to help or be like the leader.

The virtue that is the antidote to greed is charity. To be selflessly generous in one's giving to others, and to the world, would appear to counter greedy impulses. Harper (2017) goes further in suggesting that *accountability* is the best antidote to greed. Accountability, argues Harper, ensures that "you're doing business the way it ought to be done. The word 'ought' implies high ethical standards. It is doing the right thing, in the right way, with the right motives" (p. 1). Harper recommends that leaders foster both *horizontal* and *vertical* accountability, with the former referring to accountability within one's leadership team and the latter referring to accountability involving those above and below the leader in the organizational chain of command. Harper maintains that "when you commit to the practice of accountability – to do the right thing, in the right way, with the right motives – you're able to shine a light on greed, defuse its power, and put your company on a solid ethical foundation" (p. 1). One problem with CEO leaders and superstars is that they negotiate golden parachutes that shield them from negative consequences of their own bad actions, intentional or not (New York Times, 2008).

Sins of the Body: Sloth, Gluttony, and Lust

We combine these last three deadly sins into one category, as they are sins associated with bodily urges and pleasures. Sloth is defined as laziness and idleness, and Dante took it a step further by referring to sloth as the failure to love. In the realm of leadership, sloth is manifest as a failure to act when action is necessary. A leader who fails to take appropriate action when it is needed has abdicated responsibility to ensure the well-being of their followers. Leadership sloth may reflect cowardice, social loafing, and a sense of entitlement.

A modern-day example of leadership sloth occurred on January 13, 2012, when the luxury cruise ship *Costa Concordia* struck a rock formation on the floor of the Mediterranean Sea when it ventured too close to the Italian coast. The captain of the ship, Francesco Schettino, steered it toward the coast to allow a crew member to wave to friends on shore. The ship ran aground and Schettino made the error of waiting forty minutes before issuing the order to abandon ship. This inaction was later cited as a major reason for the deaths of thirty-four people and injuries to sixty-seven others. Compounding this error, the captain then abandoned his ship before all passengers and crew had evacuated. The Italian coastguard officer in radio contact with Schettino implored the captain to stay aboard the vessel to fulfill the duty of every ship's captain – to remain on board until every passenger's safety is ensured. The passengers aboard the *Costa Concordia* needed leadership and Schettino made himself unavailable to provide it. As a consequence of his gross misjudgment and sloth, Schettino was sentenced to ten years in prison for manslaughter, five years for causing a shipwreck, and one year for abandoning the passengers at the time of the sinking (Franco, 2017).

In stark contrast to the failed leadership of Francesco Schettino of the *Costa Concordia* disaster is the heroic leadership of Sully Sullenberger, who landed US Airways Flight 1549 on the Hudson River on January 25, 2009. Shortly after takeoff, Captain Sullenberger's jet hit a flock of Canada geese, disabling both engines. Unable to reach another airport, Sullenberger improvised a "landing" on the Hudson River. Passengers and crew stood on the wings of the floating aircraft, waiting for boats to rescue them. Sullenberger was the last person to leave the plane, and twice he made sweeps through the cabin to ensure that every passenger and crew member had safely evacuated. All 155 people on board survived the incident, thanks to Sullenberger's good judgment and *diligence* – the trait that is the antidote to sloth.

The final two sins of gluttony and lust were described by Dante (Alighieri 1320/2009) as "excessive love of pleasure" (canto 6, line 97) and "excessive love of others" (canto 5, line 113), respectively. There is no shortage of leaders in politics and in the entertainment industry who have sabotaged their careers, and many times lost their lives, because of their inability to contain their love for the sensual pleasures of food, sex, and drugs. In politics, the alcohol abuse of Ulysses S. Grant and Ted Kennedy is well known. Sex scandals have rocked the political careers of Bill Clinton, Gary Hart, Herman Cain, Eliot Spitzer, Anthony Weiner, John Edwards, and Newt Gingrich. The #MeToo movement has identified dozens of prominent offenders who placed the fulfillment of sensual pleasures ahead of their careers and, more importantly, the well-being of their victims (Beggan, 2019b).

Sexual misconduct usually ends careers, not lives. Alcohol and drug addiction, however, has claimed the lives of scores of legendary leaders in the entertainment field. A partial list of those who have tragically succumbed to the pleasures of sex, drugs, or food includes Elvis Presley, Whitney Houston, River Phoenix, Michael Jackson, Chris Farley, John Belushi, Jimi Hendrix, Janis Joplin, Prince, and Heath Ledger. There are hundreds if not thousands more names of the rich and famous who we could list. Deadly addiction is a terrible problem for all of humanity, not just for leadership.

Two heroic leaders in finding solutions to addictive behavior have been Betty Ford and Bill Wilson. Betty Ford was the First Lady and wife of former President Gerald Ford. Throughout much of her adult life, she battled addictions with prescription drugs and alcohol. Most public figures of her era kept their demons in private, but in the 1970s Betty Ford "outed" herself as an addict and publicly enrolled in a rehab clinic. Later, she established the Betty Ford Center, a residential treatment facility for people with substance abuse challenges. She showed heroic leadership in admitting her addictions in public and in demonstrating the courage to identify all addictions not as a moral failing but as a treatable physical and psychological problem.

Incorruptibility As the Greatest Power

Philosophers, ethicists, and scholars have long debated the question of which virtue is the greatest of them all. Some have argued that the ultimate virtue is kindness (Malti, 2021). For others, it is humility (Worthington & Allison, 2018), truth and honesty (Wilson, 2018), gratitude (Wood, Froh, & Geraghty, 2010), self-control (Alalade, 2022), or courage (Ju, 2008). Allison and Goethals (2011) found that most people consider selflessness to be the greatest of all the heroic traits. In positive psychology, researchers have found that zest, hope, and humor are the three character strengths most often found in psychologically mature and healthy people (Gander et al., 2022).

Is the virtue of *incorruptibility* the panacea for the seven deadly sins? In a recent essay, Hutchins (in press) makes this argument. While acknowledging the truth of Lord Acton's dictum, that possessing power over others is dangerous, Hutchins also argues that people have the power to resist the corrosive, corrupting influence of power. All humans have the power of incorruptibility, argues Hutchins, echoing the sentiment of heroism scholars, who believe in the *banality of heroism* – the idea that all people are capable of becoming heroes (Franco & Zimbardo, 2006). Hutchins (in press) makes the case that incorruptibility may be the greatest of all human powers. That is, it may be the pinnacle of virtue.

We are not aware of anyone but Hutchins (in press) who has argued that incorruptibility is the greatest virtue, despite the fact that, throughout human history, it is an indisputable fact that hundreds of millions of innocent people have died at the hands of political and religious leaders who allowed power to corrupt them (Tams, Berster, & Schiffbauer, 2014). A leader who demonstrates incorruptibility may do more to promote and preserve human life than a leader who displays all other highly valued human virtues combined.

Once again, we turn to fiction storytelling to illustrate the power of incorruptibility. Consider the comic book superhero Superman. He had nearly limitless power. He was super strong, could fly through walls, possessed X-ray vision, and could move faster than the speed of light (in defiance of relativity theory). He could melt lead just by looking at it, and his breath was more powerful than hurricane winds. Bullets and lasers bounced harmlessly off his body, and he could fly through the sun without harm. If ever a being had absolute power, it was Superman.

But consider how Superman lived his life. The most powerful being in the universe worked as an anonymous reporter, disguised as a mild-mannered everyman, bullied by his boss, and rebuffed by the women at the office. His personal time was spent in his Fortress of Solitude in quiet contemplation among the souvenirs and mementos of his extraordinary life. He could have had any woman he wanted, by force or charisma, and he could have had any riches that he desired. Superman could have ruled the world, for no one had the ability to deny him anything. But instead, he used his power to protect the planet, to defend the defenseless, to uplift the downtrodden, and even to rescue cats who were stuck in trees. Superman is the ultimate illustration of the greatest power of incorruptibility. He used great humility to prevent himself from being the hazard his great power could have made him.

Real-world leaders have also shown the virtue of incorruptibility. George Washington, one of the founders of the United States, would be the first to admit of his errors and failings; yet he is characterized by his numerous demonstrations of incorruptibility. Washington wrote, "As the first of everything in our situation will serve to establish a precedent, it is devoutly wished on my part that these precedents be fixed on true principles" (Rozell, Pederson, & Williams, 2000, p. 146). Therefore, rather than be addressed as royalty, as recommended by Congress and his Cabinet, he preferred the more humble honorific "Mr. President." Fearing that too much power could fall into his own hands, Washington established a group of advisors to the president called the Cabinet and declined a third term in office – a precedent that lasted more than a century and is now mandated by the Twenty-Second Amendment to the US Constitution. He also preferred that the president receive no salary and that the United States have no political parties, but he did not get his way on these matters.

Closer to our own time, we can still find examples of incorruptibility. In the 1960s, when the United States was involved in an unpopular war in Vietnam, many people, especially men of draft age, fled to Canada or other foreign countries or simply went underground to avoid serving. This was a matter of conscience for people who opposed the war. However, some others, notably the heavyweight boxing champion Muhammed Ali, chose to defy the draft and face the consequences in order to more forcefully make their point. Ali was arrested and convicted of draft evasion. Moreover, he was stripped of his boxing titles and would have served five years in prison if the Supreme Court had not overturned his conviction (Ali, 2015). By not taking the easy way out and taking the fall for his beliefs, he became an inspiration to Americans and an international icon.

Incorruptibility may be the greatest and the rarest of virtues. It is an indispensable quality for heroic leaders to possess, as it enables leaders to resist the temptation to abuse their power. We may live in an age of incivility and chaos, when the foundations of our civilization are ignored and shaken, but it is still possible to find people with integrity. As political ideologies veer ever more to the extremes, a handful of politicians will risk ostracism to stand by their beliefs. In a society where ignorance and anti-intellectualism increasingly become admirable traits, there are still journalists, comedians, and laypeople who will call out the hypocrisy and double standards of our society. Most of all, there are unsung heroes all around the world, making heroic choices anonymously, who will defy temptations to act on pride, greed, envy, and wrath. Hutchins (in press) makes a compelling point: Everyone has the potential to demonstrate heroic leadership because everyone has the power to be incorruptible.

Conclusion

We return to Lord Acton's observation that great people are bad people. This Element has underscored the fine line between greatness and badness, a line that great leaders can cross easily without their awareness. Equally alarming, the line can even be crossed without the awareness of the leader's followers. We have suggested that the seven deadly sins provide a useful framework for understanding why great leadership can become a hazard.

Lord Acton knew that absolute power can operate as a type of pharmaceutical potion that distorts the thoughts, emotions, and behaviors of the leader along with the entire group, organization, or nation that is being led. Great leaders can have the most noble of intentions and yet deliver terrible destruction. With surprising ease, heroic leadership can slip into villainous leadership, and evidence for this slippage is found in research on evil showing that the vast majority of villains believe they are heroes doing good, not villains doing bad (Baumeister, 2012).

As social psychologists, the authors of this Element are all too aware of the myriad ways that a psychological phenomenon such as leadership can express itself in nonobvious, counterintuitive ways. *Psychology is not common sense.* Consider the unquestioned law of nature that the more behavior is positively reinforced, the more likely it is to be repeated. Psychologists have also found the opposite to be true under a set of fairly common circumstances (Lepper, Greene, & Nisbett, 1973). Consider the truism that birds of a feather flock together. Psychologists have found that sometimes opposites attract (Kristof-Brown, Barrick, & Stevens, 2005).

The three authors of this Element have each published work that illuminates reversals of so-called common-sense psychology. The lead author, James

Beggan, has published an influential article on "the downside of heroism" (Beggan, 2019a). In this article, Beggan argues persuasively that heroes can sometimes, and unknowingly, do more harm than good. The second author, Scott Allison, has published work showing that great leadership is filled with paradoxes and contradictions (Allison & Cecilione, 2016). The third author, George Goethals, has published work demonstrating the counterintuitive idea that ambiguous and mysterious information can be more useful to leaders than clear, concrete information (Goethals & Allison, 2019).

During the latter half of our careers, we have been devoted to helping leaders gain an awareness of biases in perception and judgment that produce disastrous outcomes. People confuse a long list of principles and phenomena with great leadership. Charisma is one such false indicator of greatness. People also harbor the false belief that fame and celebrity status are diagnostic of wisdom and effectiveness in a leader. Goethals and Allison (in press) have called this the *heroism attribution error*. Wealth is also the fool's gold of great leadership, especially in Western cultures that worship money and materialism. Good looks are also deceptive, as people tend to believe that physical attractiveness denotes intelligence, morality, and wisdom (Eagly et al., 1991). We believe that the more leaders and followers are made aware of these and other biases, the less likely they will succumb to them.

The assertion that great leadership can be a hazard to leaders, followers, the organization itself, and the larger society in which the organization exists contradicts the widely accepted belief that great leaders are one factor that has allowed the human race to achieve greatness. The reason that great leadership can be a hazard is that it operates in ways that can tempt people to behave in self-serving ways that may run counter to the goals of great leadership, which involve prosocial or even altruistic motives that allow people to attain new heights and new achievements. Processes associated with great leadership can influence leaders to become uninhibited and self-focused and followers to become lazy and superficial in their thinking.

We have used the seven deadly sins to outline the numerous ways in which even great leadership can fail. These sins affect human beings through the operation of ordinary social psychological principles, which explains at least in part why it may be so difficult to fight against them. We use the word "tempt" because it is consistent with our decision to apply the seven deadly sins in understanding why great leadership can become a hazard. However, it is important to note that a temptation is viewed as an intentional – though perhaps impulsive – response to an attractive but ultimately undesirable or unwise choice. As we have outlined in our discussion of the phenomenon of the hazard of great leadership, it is true that in some cases leaders intentionally make decisions knowing that they represent the first steps on the royal road to ruin. These decisions might involve putting self-gain ahead of the overall well-being of an institution or actually engaging in self-dealing or criminal acts. In other cases, however, the hazard of great leadership comes about because of features of the human condition that do not involve faults of a leader. One of the best examples of this involves the tendency of followers to engage in social loafing in response to a too-competent leader. Inaction on the part of followers based on the leader's extreme success should not be viewed as a frailty of leadership.

As noted by Baumeister et al. (2001, p. 323), "Bad is stronger than good." By extension, it is possible that bad leadership might be stronger than good leadership. That is, a bad leader may be more readily able to destroy an organization than a good leader could promote or heal it. Although a provocative sentiment, evidence based on a meta-analysis does not support this conclusion (Schyns & Schilling, 2013). However, our conceptual analysis suggests that even apparently positive leadership can have unexpected negative consequences. Further, we have outlined a number of psychological processes to explain why great leaders can be hazards. Additional effort is called for to determine the extent to which researchers may be able to obtain empirical evidence of the hazard posed by great leadership.

According to Taylor (1991, p. 67), a negative event "has the potential or actual ability to create adverse outcomes for the individual. Thus, the definition includes events that have not occurred but are perceived as potentially threatening, as well as those that have occurred and are perceived as harmful." A trauma is a single bad event that has a prolonged, negative effect on the recipient. In other words, a trauma is a very significant bad event. As noted by Baumeister et al. (2001, p. 327), "Many kinds of traumas produce severe and lasting effects on behavior, but there is no corresponding concept of a positive event that can have similarly strong and lasting effects. In a sense, trauma has no true opposite concept."

The potential impact of extreme, negative events is relevant to our analysis of the potential hazard posed by great leadership. To be a great leader, someone may have to do many things right. To be a bad leader, it might be possible to do just one thing extremely badly. Thus, given the many actions that a leader must take, from a simple probabilistic perspective, great leadership is difficult because it requires the intersection of many positive traits and events. Bad leadership is much easier, however, because one bad day – or bad decision – may be enough to contaminate a leader's influence.

The current rise of cancel culture, which "has seemed to evolve from a once online ethos of 'outing' politically incorrect celebrities into an umbrella philosophy that has fused seemingly disparate movements like 'Me Too,' Black

Lives Matter and even ANTIFA" (Duque, Rivera, & LeBlanc, 2021, p. 11), illustrates how a single bad decision can have serious deleterious effects on a person or organization. Further, cancel culture may inhibit minority opinions on the Left or the Right (Norris, 2023) and is consistent with the *spiral of silence theory*, which states that people are sensitive to how many people share their opinion and will become less inclined to voice their views if they feel they are in the minority (Noelle-Neumann, 1991). This chilling effect can produce a cascade such that fewer and fewer people become willing to speak out against what they perceive to be a majority because they are unaware of other dissenters.

Although we have argued that great (or even merely good) leaders may inadvertently do harm to their organizations, an underlying assumption of our approach is that leaders matter – regardless of whether the influence is good or bad. An alternative and even more subversive approach is to assert that leaders may have less impact than is popularly assumed. Interestingly, if we assume that leaders have less positive impact than we assume, it is also possible that they may have less negative influence than we assume. What would be unfortunate – and the subject of future empirical investigation – is that great leaders may have less impact than we assume in making an organization great but more influence than we assume in making an organization inferior. Their influence in the negative domain may stem from assumptions we make about the influence of great leaders, including a failure to recognize how the seven deadly sins may interfere with the performance and accomplishments of even great leaders.

A specific leader may be less influential in bringing about organizational outcomes than might be expected because of constraints that operate on leaders (Pfeffer, 1977). Leaders or potential leaders may be relatively homogeneous as a group. This low level of variability is potentially because leaders self-select into a position of wanting to be a leader. Further, those who select a leader may use a relatively narrow set of criteria. In other words, there may be a leader stereotype invoked by those selecting a leader. Potential candidates who fail to match the stereotype may self-select out of consideration. Selection committees may also exclude them.

Another constraint that limits leader behavior is the system in which the leader is embedded. Leaders may be limited by legal, cultural, and bureaucratic factors that constrain their ability to make decisions or propose or act upon policies. A third constraint that operates on leaders are macro-level social, economic, and environmental conditions that limit a leader's ability to enact policies. Although it is possible that some leaders may be better at anticipating or coping with these external constraints, these individual differences may be outweighed by the magnitude of the external influence itself.

Our tendency to attribute great importance to leaders may be related to the *supernatural punishment hypothesis* (Johnson & Krüger, 2004), which states that the fear of punishment from a supernatural being – regardless of whether it is real – is enough to encourage cooperative behavior. In support of the supernatural punishment hypothesis, Johnson (2005) found that a belief in "high gods" concerned with human morality was associated with more cooperation in 186 societies in the world. A belief in a morally restrictive supernatural entity may provide an evolutionary advantage (Johnson, 2009).

The tendency to look for great leaders may relate to a belief in a supernatural being who governs how people should behave. Deferring to a leader would tend to reduce interpersonal conflict. Of course, this relationship could be sabotaged by a leader who does not endorse morally correct behavior or, perhaps worse, does so for others but not for himself or herself. Ultimately, this double standard might fuel resentment if recognized or interfere with the optimal functioning of a leader–follower system, even if followers are unaware of its operation.

As noted by Johnson (2009, p. 178), "a belief in God, even if false, may be favored by natural selection if its costs are less than those of assuming one is alone and free to do as one wishes. A fear of the fires of hell may be a very effective smoke alarm against getting burnt for real in this world." As an extension, it is also possible that the tendency to romance leadership (Meindl, 1995) – to see a leader as better than reality would indicate – might be related to the tendency to believe in the supernatural. According to Johnson (2009, pp. 169–170), "supernatural beliefs may have been an effective mindguard against excessively selfish behaviour."

Our analysis focused on the way in which leaders can inadvertently harm themselves and their organizations and drew attention to the limitations of leaders. By extension, the field of leadership studies has made the leader the central focus of its study. We argue that a discipline that places too much emphasis on a single explanatory construct limits itself. That is why we welcome research that considers an expanded view of the leadership dynamic, which includes the importance of the study of followership, for example.

References

Acton, J. E. E. D. (1949). Acton–Creighton correspondence. In G. Himmelfarb (Ed.), *Essays on freedom and power* (pp. 357–373). Boston, MA: Beacon Press.

Adler, M. (1985). Stardom and talent. *The American Economic Review, 75*(1), 208–212.

Adorno, T. W., Frenkel-Brunswik, E., Levinson, D. J., & Sanford, R. N. (1950). *The authoritarian personality.* New York: Harper & Brothers.

Alalade (2022). Self-control: The basis of all virtues. [Online]. www.abuad.edu .ng/self-control-the-basis-of-all-virtues/.

Ali, M. (2015). *The greatest: My own story.* Los Angeles, CA: Graymalkin Media.

Alighieri, D. (1320/2009). *The divine comedy* (trans. H. F. Cary). Ware: Wordsworth Editions.

Allison, S. T., & Cecilione, J. L. (2016). Paradoxical truths in heroic leadership: Implications for leadership development and effectiveness. In R. Bolden, M. Witzel, & N. Linacre (Eds.), *Leadership paradoxes* (pp. 73–92). London: Routledge.

Allison, S. T., & Goethals, G. R. (2011). *Heroes: What they do and why we need them.* New York: Oxford University Press.

Allison, S. T., & Goethals, G. R. (2016). Hero worship: The elevation of the human spirit. *Journal for the Theory of Social Behaviour, 46*(2), 187–210.

Allison, S. T., Goethals, G. R., & Spyrou, S. P. (2020). Donald Trump as the archetypal *puer aeternus*: The psychology of mature and immature leadership. In K. Bezio & G. R. Goethals (Eds.), *Leadership, populism, and resistance* (pp. 160–175). Northampton, MA: Edward Elgar.

Al-Nasour, J., & Najm, N. A. (2020). Leadership capital: Concept and roles. *Economics and Management, 17*(1), 120–126.

Alvesson, M. (2019). Waiting for Godot: Eight major problems in the odd field of leadership studies. *Leadership, 15*(1), 27–43.

Anderson, A. A., Yeo, S. K., Brossard, D., Scheufele, D. A., & Xenos, M. A. (2018). Toxic talk: How online incivility can undermine perceptions of media. *International Journal of Public Opinion Research, 30*(1), 156–168.

Antonakis, J. (2017). On doing better science: From thrill of discovery to policy implications. *The Leadership Quarterly, 28*(1), 5–21.

Antonakis, J., Bastardoz, N., Jacquart, P., & Shamir, B. (2016). Charisma: An ill-defined and ill-measured gift. *Annual Review of Organizational Psychology and Organizational Behavior, 3*, 293–319.

Antonakis, J., House, R. J., & Simonton, D. K. (2017). Can super smart leaders suffer from too much of a good thing? The curvilinear effect of intelligence on perceived leadership behavior. *Journal of Applied Psychology, 102*(7), 1003–1021.

Ashton, M. C., & Lee, K. (2007). Empirical, theoretical, and practical advantages of the HEXACO model of personality structure. *Personality and Social Psychology Review, 11*(2), 150–166.

Associated Press (2022). Greg Norman criticized by Australian golfers for LIV role. *ESPN*, May 19. www.espn.com/golf/story/_/id/33942187/hang-your-head-shame-greg-norman-criticized-australian-golfers-liv-role-comments-jamal-khashoggi-killing.

Baker, R., & Benner, K. (2022). Jan. 6 committee appears to lay out road map for prosecuting Trump. *New York Times*, June 11. www.nytimes.com/2022/06/11/us/politics/jan-6-prosecute-trump.html.

Barnes, D. F. (1978). Charisma and religious leadership: An historical analysis. *Journal for the Scientific Study of Religion, 17*(1), 1–18.

Baumeister, R. F. (2012). Human evil: The myth of pure evil and the true causes of violence. In M. Mikulincer & P. R. Shaver (Eds.), *The social psychology of morality* (pp. 367–380). Washington, DC: American Psychological Association.

Baumeister, R. F., Bratslavsky, E., Finkenauer, C., & Vohs, K. D. (2001). Bad is stronger than good. *Review of General Psychology, 5*(4), 323–370.

Baumeister, R. F., Campbell, J. D., Krueger, J. I., & Vohs, K. D. (2003). Does high self-esteem cause better performance, interpersonal success, happiness, or healthier lifestyles? *Psychological Science in the Public Interest, 4*(1), 1–44.

Beggan, J. K. (2019a). On the downside of heroism: Grey zone limitations on the value of social and physical risk heroism. *Heroism Science, 4*, 1–35.

Beggan, J. K. (2019b). *Sexual harassment, the abuse of power and the crisis of leadership: "Superstar" harassers and how to stop them.* Northampton, MA: Edward Elgar.

Black, S. (2016). Opinion: Saints or sinnners: Where to for whistleblowers? *LSJ: Law Society of NSW Journal, 19*(February), 24–25.

Bligh, M. C., Kohles, J. C., & Pillai, R. (2011). Romancing leadership: Past, present, and future. *The Leadership Quarterly, 22*(6), 1058–1077.

Block, S. R. (2004). *Why nonprofits fail: Overcoming founder's syndrome, fundphobia, and other obstacles to success.* San Francisco, CA: Jossey-Bass.

Block, S. R., & Rosenberg, S. (2002). Toward an understanding of founder's syndrome: An assessment of power and privilege among founders of nonprofit organizations. *Nonprofit Management and Leadership*, *12*(4), 353–368.

Bok, D. (1993). *The cost of talent: How executives and professionals are paid and how it affects America*. New York: Free Press.

Bolden, R., Witzel, M., & Linacre, N. (2016). *Leadership paradoxes: Rethinking leadership for an uncertain world*. London: Routledge.

Bostock, B. (2020). Michael Cohen says Trump hates Obama because he's jealous. *Insider*, September 9. www.businessinsider.com/michael-cohen-trump-jealous-obama-rachel-maddow-2020-9.

Boyatzis, R. E. (2011). Managerial and leadership competencies: A behavioral approach to emotional, social and cognitive intelligence. *Vision*, *15*(2), 91–100.

Brandes, L., Franck, E., & Nüesch, S. (2008). Local heroes and superstars: An empirical analysis of star attraction in German soccer. *Journal of Sports Economics*, *9*(3), 266–286.

Brienes, J. (2013). Five ways to ease your envy. *Greater Good*, August 1. https://greatergood.berkeley.edu/article/item/five_ways_to_ease_your_envy.

Brookhiser, R. (1996). A man on horseback. *Atlantic Monthly*, *277*(1), 50–64.

Brown, J. D., & Marshall, M. A. (2001). Great expectations: Optimism and pessimism in achievement settings. In E. C. Chang (Ed.), *Optimism and pessimism: Implications for theory, research, and practice* (pp. 239–255). Washington, DC: American Psychological Association.

Brown, L. (2022). *Hidden secrets of Buddhism*. Miami, FL: Buddha's Heart Press.

Bruine de Bruin, W., Parker, A. M., & Fischhoff, B. (2020). Decision-making competence: More than intelligence? *Current Directions in Psychological Science*, *29*(2), 186–192.

Bruschke, J., & Divine, L. (2017). Debunking Nixon's radio victory in the 1960 election: Re-analyzing the historical record and considering currently unexamined polling data. *The Social Science Journal*, *54*(1), 67–75.

Burns, J. M. (1978). *Leadership*. New York: Harper & Row.

Buyl, T., Boone, C., & Wade, J. B. (2019). CEO narcissism, risk-taking, and resilience: An empirical analysis in US commercial banks. *Journal of Management*, *45*(4), 1372–1400.

Callan, S. (2003). Charismatic leadership in contemporary management debates. *Journal of General Management*, *29*(1), 1–14.

Campbell, W. K., Bonacci, A. M., Shelton, J., Exline, J. J., & Bushman, B. J. (2004). Psychological entitlement: Interpersonal consequences and validation of a self-report measure. *Journal of Personality Assessment, 83*(1), 29–45.

Carlyle, T. (1841). *On heroes, hero-worship and the heroic in history.* London: James Fraser.

Chait, J. (2021). Trump wanted to erase Obama's legacy: He failed. *Intelligencer*, January 18. https://nymag.com/intelligencer/2021/01/trump-wanted-to-erase-obamas-legacy-he-failed.html.

Chan, H. F., Mixon, F. G., & Torgler, B. (2019). Fame in the sciences: A culturomics approach. *Scientometrics, 118*(2), 605–615.

Cillizza, C. (2022). Why you should hit pause on the "Mike Pence is a hero" storyline. *CNN*, June 17. www.cnn.com/2022/06/17/politics/mike-pence-jan uary-6-hearing-dan-quayle.

Conger, J. A., & Kanungo, R. N. (1987). Toward a behavioral theory of charismatic leadership in organizational settings. *Academy of Management Review, 12*(4), 637–647.

Coombs, C. H., & Avrunin, G. S. (1977). Single-peaked functions and the theory of preference. *Psychological Review, 84*(2), 216–230.

Corbett, M. (2015). From law to folklore: Work stress and the Yerkes–Dodson Law. *Journal of Managerial Psychology, 30*(6), 741–752.

Costa, P. T., & McCrae, R. R. (1992). Normal personality assessment in clinical practice: The NEO Personality Inventory. *Psychological Assessment, 4*(1), 5–13.

Coughenour, C., Abelar, J., Pharr, J., Lung-Chang, C., & Singh, A. (2020). Estimated car cost as a predictor of driver yielding behaviors for pedestrians. *Journal of Transport and Health, 16*, 100831.

Cowen, A. P., King, A. W., & Marcel, J. J. (2016). CEO severance agreements: A theoretical examination and research agenda. *Academy of Management Review, 41*(1), 151–169.

Cowen, T. (2000). *What price fame?* Cambridge, MA: Harvard University Press.

de Cremer, D., & van Dijk, E. (2005). When and why leaders put themselves first: Leader behaviour in resource allocations as a function of feeling entitled. *European Journal of Social Psychology, 35*(4), 553–563.

de Cremer, D., & van Knippenberg, D. (2002). How do leaders promote cooperation? The effects of charisma and procedural fairness. *Journal of Applied Psychology, 87*(5), 858–866.

Dion, K., Berscheid, E., & Walster, E. (1972). What is beautiful is good. *Journal of Personality and Social Psychology, 24*(3), 285–290.

Druckman, J. N. (2003). The power of television images: The first Kennedy–Nixon debate revisited. *Journal of Politics, 65*(2), 559–571.

Duque, R. B., Rivera, R., & LeBlanc, E. J. (2021). The Active Shooter paradox: Why the rise of Cancel Culture, "Me Too", ANTIFA and Black Lives Matter . . . matters. *Aggression and Violent Behavior, 60,* 101544.

Eagly, A. H., Ashmore, R. D., Makhijani, M. G., & Longo, L. C. (1991). What is beautiful is good, but . . . : A meta-analytic review of research on the physical attractiveness stereotype. *Psychological Bulletin, 110*(1), 109–128.

Eagly, A. H., & Chin, J. L. (2010). Diversity and leadership in a changing world. *American Psychologist, 65*(3), 216–224.

Eavis, P. & Krauss, C. (2021). What's really behind corporate promises on climate change. *New York Times,* February 22. www.nytimes.com/2021/02/22/business/energy-environment/corporations-climate-change.html.

Ehrhart, M. G., & Klein, K. J. (2001). Predicting followers' preferences for charismatic leadership: The influence of follower values and personality. *The Leadership Quarterly, 12*(2), 153–179.

Einarsen, S., Aasland, M. S., & Skogstad, A. (2007). Destructive leadership behaviour: A definition and conceptual model. *The Leadership Quarterly, 18*(3), 207–216.

Einola, K., & Alvesson, M. (2021). When "good" leadership backfires: Dynamics of the leader/follower relation. *Organization Studies, 42*(6), 845–865.

Emrich, C. G. (1999). Context effects in leadership perception. *Personality and Social Psychology Bulletin, 25*(8), 991–1006.

Eskow, R. (2013). Six signs our culture is sick with greed. *Travel Impact Newswire,* December 5. www.travel-impact-newswire.com/2013/12/6-signs-our-culture-is-sick-with-greed-alternet/.

Ewers, J. B. (2020). Donald Trump will always envy President Barack Obama. *Amsterdam News,* February 27. https://amsterdamnews.com/news/2020/02/27/donald-trump-will-always-envy-president-barack-oba/.

Farley, R., & Robertson, L. (2017). The facts on crowd size. *Factcheck.org.* www.factcheck.org/2017/01/the-facts-on-crowd-size/

Fast, N. J., & Tiedens, L. Z. (2010). Blame contagion: The automatic transmission of self-serving attributions. *Journal of Experimental Social Psychology, 46*(1), 97–106.

Fein, S., Goethals, G. R., & Kugler, M. B. (2007). Social influence on political judgments: The case of presidential debates. *Political Psychology, 28*(2), 165–192.

Felfe, J., & Petersen, L. E. (2007). Romance of leadership and management decision making. *European Journal of Work and Organizational Psychology, 16*(1), 1–24.

Festinger, L. (1954). A theory of social comparison processes. *Human Relations, 7*(2), 117–140.

Finkelstein, J. H., & Wilde, J. A. (2017). Does your president have a platinum parachute? *Inside Higher Ed*, June 1. www.insidehighered.com/advice/2017/06/01/examination-college-presidents-platinum-parachutes-essay.

Fiske, S. T. (1993). Controlling other people: The impact of power on stereotyping. *American Psychologist*, *48*(6), 621–628.

Franco, Z. E. (2017). Heroism in times of crisis: Understanding leadership during extreme events. In S. T. Allison, G. R. Goethals, & R. M. Kramer (Eds.), *Handbook of heroism and heroic leadership*. New York: Routledge.

Franco, Z. E., & Zimbardo, P. G. (2006). The banality of heroism. *The Greater Good*, *3*, 30–35.

Freud, S. (1922). *Group psychology and the analysis of the ego*. New York: Norton & Co.

Fromm, E. (1992). *The anatomy of human destructiveness*. New York: Holt Paperbacks.

Fuchs, S. (2001). *Against essentialism: A theory of culture and society*. Cambridge, MA: Harvard University Press.

Fuller, S. R., & Aldag, R. J. (1998). Organizational Tonypandy: Lessons from a quarter century of the groupthink phenomenon. *Organizational Behavior and Human Decision Processes*, *73*(2–3), 163–184.

Fuqua, D. R., & Newman, J. L. (2004). Moving beyond the great leader model. *Consulting Psychology Journal: Practice and Research*, *56*(3), 146–153.

Galinsky, A. D., Magee, J. C., Inesi, M. E., & Gruenfeld, D. H. (2006). Power and perspectives not taken. *Psychological Science*, *17*(12), 1068–1074.

Gander, F., Wagner, L., Amann, L. & Ruch, W. (2022). What are character strengths good for? A daily diary study on character strengths enactment. *The Journal of Positive Psychology*, *17*(22), 718–728.

Gardner, H. (1983). *Frames of mind: The theory of multiple intelligences*. New York: Basic Books.

Gardner, H. (1993). *Multiple intelligences: New horizons*. New York: Basic Books.

Gert, B., & Gert, J. (2020). The definition of morality. In E. N. Zalta (Ed.), *The Stanford encyclopedia of philosophy*. https://plato.stanford.edu/archives/fall2020/entries/morality-definition/.

Gilbert, D. T., & Malone, P. S. (1995). The correspondence bias. *Psychological Bulletin*, *117*(1), 21–38.

Gino, F., Ayal, S., & Ariely, D. (2009). Contagion and differentiation in unethical behavior: The effect of one bad apple on the barrel. *Psychological Science*, *20*(3), 393–398.

Gladwell, M. (2005). *Blink: The power of thinking without thinking.* New York: Little, Brown and Company.

Goethals, G. R. (2005). Nonverbal behavior and political leadership. In R. E. Riggio & R. S. Feldman (Eds.), *Applications of nonverbal communication* (pp. 95–115). Mahwah, NJ: Lawrence Erlbaum Associates.

Goethals, G. R., & Allison, S. T. (2012). Making heroes: The construction of courage, competence, and virtue. In J. M. Olson & M. P. Zanna (Eds.), *Advances in experimental social psychology* (Vol. 46, pp. 183–235). San Diego, CA: Elsevier.

Goethals, G. R., & Allison, S. T. (2019). *The romance of heroism and heroic leadership: Ambiguity, attribution, and apotheosis.* Bingley: Emerald.

Goethals, G. R., & Allison, S. T. (in press). The construction and presentation of heroes and heroines. In K. Lee (Ed.), *A cultural history of fame in the modern age.* London: Bloomsbury Press.

Goethals, G. R., & Darley, J. M. (1987). Social comparison theory: Self-evaluation and group life. In B. Mullen & G. R. Goethals (Eds.), *Theories of group behavior* (pp. 21–47). New York: Springer.

Goffee, R., & Jones, G. (2005). Managing authenticity: The paradox of great leadership. *Harvard Business Review, 83*(12), 86–94.

Graham, J., Haidt, J., Koleva, S. et al. (2013). Moral foundations theory: The pragmatic validity of moral pluralism. *Advances in experimental social psychology, 47*, 55–130.

Grant, A. M., & Schwartz, B. (2011). Too much of a good thing: The challenge and opportunity of the inverted U. *Perspectives on Psychological Science, 6*(1), 61–76.

Grant, C. (2002). Whistle blowers: Saints of secular culture. *Journal of Business Ethics, 39*(4), 391–399.

Gravley, D. (2001). Risk, hazard, and disaster. [Online]. https://homepages.uc .edu/~huffwd/Volcanic_HazardRisk/Gravley.pdf.

Greenberg, J., Kosloff, S., Solomon, S., Cohen, F., & Landau, M. (2010). Toward understanding the fame game: The effect of mortality salience on the appeal of fame. *Self and Identity, 9*(1), 1–18.

Greenleaf, R. K. (1977). *Servant leadership: A journey into the nature of legitimate power and greatness.* New York: Paulist Press.

Grover, C. A., Leftwich, M. J., Backhaus, A. L., Fairchild, J. A., & Weaver, K. A. (2006). Qualities of superstar graduate students. *Teaching of Psychology, 33*(4), 271–273.

Gulati, M., & Sanchez, V. (2002). Giants in world of pygmies? Testing the superstar hypothesis with judicial opinions in casebooks. *Iowa Law Review, 87*(4), 1141–1212.

Han, D. E., & Laurent, S. M. (2023). Beautiful seems good, but perhaps not in every way: Linking attractiveness to moral evaluation through perceived vanity. *Journal of Personality and Social Psychology*, *124*(2), 264–286.

Harper, J. D. (2017). How great leaders defuse the destructive power of greed to build lasting success. *Linkedin*. www.linkedin.com/pulse/how-great-leaders-defuse-destructive-power-greed-harper-jr-chfc/.

Harrington, C. (2021). What is "toxic masculinity" and why does it matter? *Men and Masculinities*, *24*(2), 345–352.

Harvin, O., & Killey, M. (2021). Do "superstar" CEOs impair auditors' judgement and reduce fraud detection opportunities? *Journal of Forensic and Investigative Accounting*, *13*(3), 500–514.

Hausman, J. A., & Leonard, G. K. (1997). Superstars in the National Basketball Association: Economic value and policy. *Journal of Labor Economics*, *15*(4), 586–624.

Heider, F. (1958). *The psychology of interpersonal relations*. Hillsdale, NJ: Lawrence Erlbaum Associates.

Heinlein, R. A. (1961). *Stranger in a strange land*. New York: Berkley Publishing Corporation.

Hickman, G. R., & Knouse, L. E. (2020). *When leaders face personal crisis: The human side of leadership*. New York: Routledge.

Hocking, J. E., Walker, B. A., & Fink, E. L. (1982). Physical attractiveness and judgments of morality following an "immoral" act. *Psychological Reports*, *51*(1), 111–116.

Horn, J. L., & Cattell, R. B. (1966). Refinement and test of the theory of fluid and crystallized general intelligences. *Journal of Educational Psychology*, *57*(5), 253–270.

Horner, M. (1997). Leadership theory: past, present and future. *Team Performance Management: An International Journal*, *3*(4), 270–287.

House, R. J., & Baetz, M. L. (1979). Leadership: Some empirical generalizations and new research directions. In B. M. Staw (Ed.), *Research in organizational behavior* (Vol. 1, pp. 399–401). Greenwich, CT: JAI Press.

House, R. J., & Howell, J. M. (1992). Personality and charismatic leadership. *The Leadership Quarterly*, *3*(2), 81–108.

Housman, M., & Minor, D. (2015). Toxic workers. Harvard Business School Working Paper (16–057).

Hutchins, R. (in press). Incorruptibility. In S. T. Allison, J. K. Beggan, & G. R. Goethals (Eds.), *Encyclopedia of heroism studies*. New York: Springer.

Ingersoll, Robert G. (1915). The Great Infidels. *The Works of Robert G. Ingersoll, in twelve volumes, volume III*. New York: The Dresden Publishing Company.

Johnson, D. D. P. (2005). God's punishment and public goods: A test of the supernatural punishment hypothesis in 186 world cultures. *Human Nature*, *16*(4), 410–446.

Johnson, D. D. P. (2009). The error of God: Error management theory, religion, and the evolution of cooperation. In S. A. Levin (Ed.), *Games, groups, and the global good* (pp. 169–180). Berlin: Springer.

Johnson, D. D. P., & Krüger, O. (2004). The good of wrath: Supernatural punishment and the evolution of cooperation. *Political Theology*, *5*(2), 159–176.

Ju, A. (2008). Courage is the most important virtue, says writer and civil rights activist Maya Angelou at Convocation. *Cornell Chronicle*, May 24. https://news.cornell.edu/stories/2008/05/courage-most-important-virtue-maya-angelou-tells-seniors.

Kalshoven, K., Den Hartog, D. N., & De Hoogh, A. H. B. (2011). Ethical leader behavior and big five factors of personality. *Journal of Business Ethics*, *100*(2), 349–366.

Kaplan, S., & Garrick, B. J. (1981). On the quantitative definition of risk. *Risk Analysis*, *1*(1), 11–27.

Karau, S. J. (2020). Preface. In S. J. Karau (Ed.), *Individual motivation within groups: Social loafing and motivation gains in work, academic, and sports teams* (pp. xi–xiv). Cambridge, MA: Academic Press.

Karau, S. J., & Williams, K. D. (1993). Social loafing: A meta-analytic review and theoretical integration. *Journal of Personality and Social Psychology*, *65*(4), 681–706.

Keegan, J. (1987). *The mask of command*. New York: Penguin Books.

Kellerman, B. (2004). *Bad leadership: What it is, how it happens, why it matters*. Boston, MA: Harvard Business School Press.

Kelley, B. (2019). Why Phil Mickelson was sometimes called "FIGJAM," *Liveabout.com*, January 5. www.liveabout.com/phil-mickelson-a-hated-man-3971652.

Keltner, D. (2016). Don't let power corrupt you. *Harvard Business Review*, *94*(10), 112–115. https://hbr.org/2016/10/dont-let-power-corrupt-you.

Kershaw, C., Rast, D. E., III, Hogg, M. A., & van Knippenberg, D. (2021). Battling ingroup bias with effective intergroup leadership. *British Journal of Social Psychology*, *60*(3), 765–785.

Khurana, R. (2002). The curse of the superstar CEO. *Harvard Business Review*, *80*(9), 60–66.

Klebl, C., Luo, Y., Tan, N. P. J., Ern, J. T. P., & Bastian, B. (2021). Beauty of the beast: Beauty as an important dimension in the moral standing of animals. *Journal of Environmental Psychology*, *75*(June), 101624.

Klein, K. J., & House, R. J. (1995). On fire: Charismatic leadership and levels of analysis. *The Leadership Quarterly, 6*(2), 183–198.

Knobe, J. (2017). Cognitive science suggests that Trump makes us more accepting of the morally outrageous. *Vox*, January 10. www.vox.com/the-big-idea/2017/1/10/14220790/normalization-trump-psychology-cognitive-science.

Koehn, N. F. (2014). Great men, great pay? Why CEO compensation is sky high. *The Washington Post*, June 12. www.washingtonpost.com/opinions/great-men-great-pay-why-ceo-compensation-is-sky-high/2014/06/12/6e49d796-d227-11e3-9e25-188ebe1fa93b_story.html.

Koenig, A. M., Eagly, A. H., Mitchell, A. A., & Ristikari, T. (2011). Are leader stereotypes masculine? A meta-analysis of three research paradigms. *Psychological Bulletin, 137*(4), 616–642.

Koning, L. F., & Van Kleef, G. A. (2015). How leaders' emotional displays shape followers' organizational citizenship behavior. *The Leadership Quarterly, 26*(4), 489–501.

Kraus, S. (1996). Winners of the first 1960 televised presidential debate between Kennedy and Nixon. *Journal of Communication, 46*(4), 78–96.

Kristof-Brown, A., Barrick, M. R., & Stevens, C. K. (2005). When opposites attract: A multi-sample demonstration of complementary person-team fit on extraversion. *Journal of Personality, 73*(4), 935–958.

Kroll-Smith, J., Couch, J. S., & Couch, S. R. (1991). What is a disaster? An ecological-symbolic approach to resolving the definitional debate. *International Journal of Mass Emergencies and Disasters, 9*(3), 355–366.

Langford, C. (2022). Texas truth and reconciliation panel dissects Winter Storm Uri one year after the disaster. *Courthouse News Service*, February 15. www.courthousenews.com/texas-truth-and-reconciliation-panel-dissects-winter-storm-uri-one-year-after-the-disaster/.

Last, J. V. (2022). Mike Pence is an American hero. *The Atlantic*, June 9. www.theatlantic.com/ideas/archive/2022/06/january-6-hearings-mike-pence-service-democracy/661224/.

Lepper, M. P., Greene, D., & Nisbett, R. E. (1973). Undermining children's intrinsic interest with extrinsic reward. *Journal of Personality and Social Psychology, 28*(1), 129–137.

Letiecq, B., & Wilde, J. (2020). The costs of secret presidential searches. *GMU-AAUP* (blog), April 2. https://aaupmason.org/blog/the-costs-of-secret-presidential-searches/.

Liu, C., & Yermack, D. (2012). Where are the shareholders' mansions? CEOs' home purchases, stock sales, and subsequent company performance. In S. Boubaker, B. D. Nguyen, & D. K. Nguyen (Eds.), *Corporate governance: Recent developments and new trends* (pp. 3–28). Berlin: Springer.

Loomes, G., Starmer, C., & Sugden, R. (1992). Are preferences monotonic? Testing some predictions of regret theory. *Economica, 59*(233), 17–33.

Lucifora, C., & Simmons, R. (2003). Superstar effects in sport: Evidence from Italian soccer. *Journal of Sports Economics, 4*(1), 35–55.

Luco, A. (2014). The definition of morality: Threading the needle. *Social Theory and Practice, 40*(3), 361–387.

Lurie, D. R. (2021). Jan. 6 was just the start of radicalizing Trump's Republican party. *Daily Beast,* December 31. www.thedailybeast.com/jan-6-was-just-the-start-of-radicalizing-donald-trumps-republican-party.

Lyons, S. (2017). Wall Street at 30: Is greed still good? *The Conversation,* December 8. https://theconversation.com/wall-street-at-30-is-greed-still-good-87612.

Magee, J. C., Gruenfeld, D. H., Keltner, D. J., & Galinsky, A. D. (2005). Leadership and the psychology of power. In D. M. Messick & R. M. Kramer (Eds.), *The psychology of leadership: New perspectives and research* (pp. 275–293). Hillsdale, NJ: Lawrence Erlbaum Associates.

Malmendier, U., & Tate, G. (2009). Superstar CEOs. *The Quarterly Journal of Economics, 124*(4), 1593–1638.

Malti, T. (2021). Kindness: A perspective from developmental psychology. *European Journal of Developmental Psychology, 18*(5), 629–657.

McCoy, J., & Somer, M. (2021). Overcoming polarization. *Journal of Democracy, 32*(1), 6–21.

McCullough, D. (2002). *John Adams.* New York: Simon & Schuster.

McCurdy, C. C., & Thompson, R. P. (2011). The power of Posner: Study of prestige and influence in the federal judiciary. *Idaho Law Review, 48*(1), 49–72.

McGuire, W. J. (1973). The yin and yang of progress in social psychology: Seven koan. *Journal of Personality and Social Psychology, 26*(3), 446–456.   ·

McWilliams, M. (2016). The one weird trait that predicts whether you're a Trump supporter. *Politico,* January 17. www.politico.com/magazine/story/2016/01/donald-trump-2016-authoritarian-213533/.

Meindl, J. R. (1995). The romance of leadership as a follower-centric theory: A social constructionist approach. *The Leadership Quarterly, 6*(3), 329–341.

Meindl, J. R., Ehrlich, S. B., & Dukerich, J. M. (1985). The romance of leadership. *Administrative Science Quarterly, 30*(1), 78–102.

Merryman, A. (2018). President Trump's worst behaviors can infect us all just like the flu, according to science. *The Washington Post,* March 28. www.washingtonpost.com/news/inspired-life/wp/2018/03/29/president-trumps-worst-behavior-can-spread-among-us-just-like-the-flu-according-to-science/.

Milburn, T. W., & Billings, R. S. (1976). Decision-making perspectives from psychology: Dealing with risk and uncertainty. *American Behavioral Scientist, 20*(1), 111–126.

Moore, B. (2018). Fallibility and mourning in the analytic encounter. *Salmagundi, 197,* 182–189.

Mulcahy, K. V. (1995). Rethinking groupthink: Walt Rostow and the national security advisory process in the Johnson administration. *Presidential Studies Quarterly, 25*(2), 237–250.

Mullin, C. J., & Dunn, L. F. (2002). Using baseball card prices to measure star quality and monopsony. *Economic Inquiry, 40*(4), 620–632.

Naumann, S. E., Minsky, B. D., & Sturman, M. C. (2002). The use of the concept "entitlement" in management literature: A historical review, synthesis, and discussion of compensation policy implications. *Human Resource Management Review, 12*(1), 145–166.

Neiwert, (2017). *Alt-America: The rise of the radical right in the age of Trump.* New York: Verso.

New York Times. (2008). Crashing banks and golden parachutes. *New York Times,* September 19. www.nytimes.com/2008/09/19/opinion/19iht-edban kers.1.16308239.html.

Ni, P. (2014). *How to successfully handle narcissists.* N.p.: Preston Ni Publishing.

Nicolaou, E., & Smith, C. E. (2019). A #metoo timeline to show how far we've come – & how far we need to go. *Refinery29,* October 16. www.refinery29 .com/en-us/2018/10/212801/me-too-movement-history-timeline-year-weinstein.

Niebuhr, O., Voße, J., & Brem, A. (2016). What makes a charismatic speaker? A computer-based acoustic-prosodic analysis of Steve Jobs tone of voice. *Computers in Human Behavior, 64*(November), 366–382.

Nisbett, R. E., & Wilson, T. D. (1977). The halo effect: Evidence for unconscious alteration of judgments. *Journal of Personality and Social Psychology, 35*(4), 250–256.

Noelle-Neumann, E. (1991). The theory of public opinion: The concept of the spiral of silence. *Annals of the International Communication Association, 14*(1), 256–287.

Norris, P. (2023). Cancel culture: Myth or reality? *Political Studies, 71*(1), 145–174.

Notelovitz, G. (2021). The ugly history that will forever hurt golf's most hated man. *Foxsports,* February 1. www.foxsports.com.au/golf/golf-2021-patrick-reed-cheating-history-farmers-insurance-open/news-story/269388b71b9e4 562f5081129a78cf0c0.

Obama, M. (2016). Address at the Democratic National Convention. Monday, July 25. Philadelphia, Pennsylvania.

Osnos, E. (2017). Is political hubris an illness? *The New Yorker*, May 5. www .newyorker.com/news/daily-comment/is-political-hubris-an-illness.

Owen, D., & Davidson, J. (2009). Hubris syndrome: An acquired personality disorder? A study of US presidents and UK prime ministers over the last 100 years. *Brain*, *132*(5), 1396–1406.

Park, W. W. (2000). A comprehensive empirical investigation of the relationships among variables of the groupthink model. *Journal of Organizational Behavior*, *21*(8), 873–887.

Parrott, W. G., & Smith, R. H. (1993). Distinguishing the experiences of envy and jealousy. *Journal of Personality and Social Psychology*, *64*(6), 906–920.

O., Paul (1999). *You can't make me angry*. Torrance, CA: Capizon Publishing.

Peters, C. (2010). *Lyndon B. Johnson: The American Presidents Series*. New York: Times Series.

Peters, L. H., Hartke, D. D., & Pohlmann, J. T. (1985). Fiedler's Contingency Theory of Leadership: An application of the meta-analysis procedures of Schmidt and Hunter. *Psychological Bulletin*, *97*(2), 274–285.

Pfeffer, J. (1977). The ambiguity of leadership. *Academy of Management Review*, *2*(1), 104–112.

Porath, C. L., & Erez, A. (2007). Does rudeness really matter? The effects of rudeness on task performance and helpfulness. *Academy of Management Journal*, *50*(5), 1181–1197.

Porath, C. L., & Gerbasi, A. (2015). Does civility pay? *Organizational Dynamics*, *44*(4), 281–286.

Reeves, A. (2005). Emotional intelligence: Recognizing and regulating emotions. *AAOHN Journal*, *53*(4), 172–176.

Reyes, A. (2020). I, Trump: The cult of personality, anti-intellectualism and the post-truth era. *Journal of Language and Politics*, *19*(6), 869–892.

Riggio, R. E. (1998). Charisma. In H. S. Friedman (Ed.), *Encyclopedia of mental health* (pp. 387–396). San Diego, CA: Academic Press.

Riggio, R. E. (2009). The psychology of good and bad leadership. *Psychology Today*, October 16. www.psychologytoday.com/intl/blog/cutting-edge-leader ship/200910/the-psychology-good-and-bad-leadership?fbclid=IwAR0niV 0PPz9djzbTApZ8tt_lX6miZzIgtIOC1ovDvLIPoJ-VLZAYcNo6zMk.

Ritz, M. (2022). Golf's grinch Greg Norman. *mikeritzgolf.com* (blog), March 6. https://mikeritzgolf.com/f/golfs-grinch-greg-norman.

Rizzo, J. R., House, R. J., & Lirtzman, S. I. (1970). Role conflict and ambiguity in complex organizations. *Administrative Science Quarterly*, *15*(2), 150–163.

Robinson, E. (2019). Trump's Obama envy is getting even worse. *The Washington Post*, August 26. www.washingtonpost.com/opinions/trumps-obama-envy-is-getting-even-worse/2019/08/26/5dadc7d0-c83a-11e9-be05-f76ac4ec618c_story.html.

Rosen, S. (1981). The economics of superstars. *The American Economic Review, 71*(5), 845–858.

Ross, L. (1977). The intuitive psychologist and his shortcomings: Distortions in the attribution process. In L. Berkowitz (Ed.), *Advances in experimental social psychology* (Vol. 1, pp. 173–220). New York: Academic Press.

Rozell, M. J., Pederson, W. D., & Williams, F. J. (2000). *George Washington and the origins of the American Presidency*. Westport, CT: Praeger Publishers.

Rubin, J. (2021). Texas shows that when you cannot govern, you lie. A lot. *The Washington Post*, February 17. www.washingtonpost.com/opinions/2021/02/17/texas-shows-that-when-you-cannot-govern-you-lie-lot/.

Rudic, B., Hubner, S., & Baum, M. (2021). Hustlers, hipsters and hackers: Potential employees' stereotypes of entrepreneurial leaders. *Journal of Business Venturing Insights, 15*(June), e00220.

Rudman, L. A., Feinberg, J., & Fairchild, K. (2002). Minority members' implicit attitudes: Automatic ingroup bias as a function of group status. *Social Cognition, 20*(4), 294–320.

Rus, D., van Knippenberg, D., & Wisse, B. (2010). Leader self-definition and leader self-serving behavior. *The Leadership Quarterly, 21*(3), 509–529.

Saleem, F., Malik, M. I., & Malik, M. K. (2021). Toxic leadership and safety performance: Does organizational commitment act as stress moderator? *Cogent Business & Management, 8*(1), 1960246.

Salovey, P., & Grewal, D. (2005). The science of emotional intelligence. *Current Directions in Psychological Science, 14*(6), 281–285.

Sanchez-Hucles, J. V., & Davis, D. D. (2010). Women and women of color in leadership: Complexity, identity, and intersectionality. *American Psychologist, 65*(3), 171–181.

Schilpzand, P., De Pater, I. E., & Erez, A. (2016). Workplace incivility: A review of the literature and agenda for future research. *Journal of Organizational Behavior, 37*(S1), 57–88.

Schueller-Weidekamm, C., & Kautzky-Willer, A. (2012). Challenges of work–life balance for women physicians/mothers working in leadership positions. *Gender Medicine, 9*(4), 244–250.

Schyns, B., & Schilling, J. (2013). How bad are the effects of bad leaders? A meta-analysis of destructive leadership and its outcomes. *The Leadership Quarterly, 24*(1), 138–158.

Sedikides, C., & Strube, M. J. (1997). To thine own self be good, sure, true and better. In M. P. Zanna (Ed.), *Advances in experimental social psychology* (Vol. 29, pp. 209–269). San Diego, CA: Academic Press.

Shafer, J. (2022). The tragedy of Mike Pence. *Politico*, June 21. www.politico.com/news/magazine/2022/06/21/mike-pence-hero-00041003.

Shamir, B. (1992). Attribution of influence and charisma to the leader: The romance of leadership revisited. *Journal of Applied Social Psychology*, *22*(5), 386–407.

Simonton, D. K. (1985). Intelligence and personal influence in groups: Four nonlinear models. *Psychological Review*, *92*(4), 532–547.

Simonton, D. K. (1987). *Why presidents succeed: A political psychology of leadership*. New Haven, CT: Yale University Press.

Smith, D. (2020). "It eats him alive inside": Trump's latest attack shows endless obsession with Obama. *The Guardian*, May 16. www.theguardian.com/us-news/2020/may/16/trump-obama-obsession-coronavirus-president.

Smith, K. (2013). *Environmental hazards: Assessing risk and reducing disaster*, 6th ed. New York: Routledge.

Spector, B. A. (2016). Carlyle, Freud, and the great man theory more fully considered. *Leadership*, *12*(2), 250–260.

Staw, B. M., McKechnie, P. I., & Puffer, S. M. (1983). The justification of organizational performance. *Administrative Science Quarterly*, *28*(4), 582–600.

Stouten, J., & Liden, R. C. (2020). Social loafing in organizational work groups: The mitigating effect of servant leadership. In S. J. Karau (Ed.), *Individual motivation within groups: Social loafing and motivation gains in work, academic, and sports teams* (pp. 55–80). Cambridge, MA: Academic Press.

Strong, C., & Killingsworth, M. (2011). Stalin the charismatic leader? Explaining the "cult of personality" as a legitimation technique. *Politics, Religion & Ideology*, *12*(4), 391–411.

Sturm, R. E., Vera, D., & Crossan, M. (2017). The entanglement of leader character and leader competence and its impact on performance. *The Leadership Quarterly*, *28*(3), 349–366.

Taddonio, P. (2020). Trump the "bully": How childhood and military school shaped the future president. *Frontline*, September 22. www.pbs.org/wgbh/frontline/article/trump-the-bully-how-childhood-military-school-shaped-the-future-president/.

Tams, C. J., Berster, L., & Schiffbauer, B. (2014). *Convention on the prevention and punishment of the crime of genocide*. Oxford: Beck, Hart, Nomos Publishing.

Taylor, J. (2018). White House doctors says Trump is in "excellent" physical, cognitive health. *NPR News*, January 16. www.npr.org/2018/01/16/

578424523/white-house-doctor-says-trump-is-in-excellent-physical-cogni tive-health.

Taylor, S. E. (1991). Asymmetrical effects of positive and negative events: The mobilization-minimization hypothesis. *Psychological Bulletin, 110*(1), 67–85.

Thaler, R. H. (2017). Behavioral economics. *Journal of Political Economy, 125* (6), 1799–1805.

Thomasch, P., & Paul, F. (2008). False web report plays havoc with Apple stock. *Reuters*, October 3. www.reuters.com/article/us-apple-jobs/false-web-report-plays-havoc-with-apple-stock-idUSTRE49250A20081003.

Tilstra, D. A. (2010). Charismatic leaders as team leaders: An evaluation focused on pastoral leadership. *Journal of Religious Leadership, 9*(2), 27–55.

Tsvetkova M. & Macy, M. W. (2014). The social contagion of generosity. *PLoS ONE, 9*(2), 87275.

Turner, M. E., & Pratkanis, A. R. (1998). Twenty-five years of groupthink theory and research: Lessons from the evaluation of a theory. *Organizational Behavior and Human Decision Processes, 73*(2–3), 105–115.

Twenge, J. M., & Campbell, W. K. (2010). Birth cohort differences in the monitoring the future dataset and elsewhere: Further evidence for Generation Me – Commentary on Trzesniewski & Donnellan. *Perspectives on Psychological Science, 5*(1), 81–88.

Useem, J. (2017). Power causes brain damage. *The Atlantic*, July–August. www .theatlantic.com/magazine/archive/2017/07/power-causes-brain-damage/ 528711/.

Vancil, D. L., & Pendell, S. D. (1987). The myth of viewer–listener disagreement in the first Kennedy–Nixon debate. *Central States Speech Journal, 38* (1), 16–27.

van Dierendonck, D. (2011). Servant leadership: A review and synthesis. *Journal of Management, 37*(4), 1228–1261.

van Vugt, M., & Ronay, R. (2014). The evolutionary psychology of leadership: Theory, review, and roadmap. *Organizational Psychology Review, 4*(1), 74–95.

Vaughan, D. (1996). *The Challenger launch decision: Risky technology, culture, and deviance at NASA*. Chicago, IL: University of Chicago Press.

Vergauwe, J., Wille, B., Hofmans, J., Kaiser, R. B., & De Fruyt, F. (2018). The double-edged sword of leader charisma: Understanding the curvilinear relationship between charismatic personality and leader effectiveness. *Journal of Personality and Social Psychology, 114*(1), 110–130.

von Hippel, W. (2018). *The social leap*. New York: Harperwave.

von Hippel, W., Ronay, R., Baker, E., Kjelsaas, K., & Murphy, S. C. (2016). Quick thinkers are smooth talkers: Mental speed facilitates charisma. *Psychological Science, 27*(1), 119–122.

Waldman, P. (2021). Insane GOP lies about Texas offer a depressing preview of coming climate debates. *The Washington Post,* February 17. www .washingtonpost.com/opinions/2021/02/17/insane-gop-lies-about-texas-offer-depressing-preview-coming-climate-debates/?itid=lk_inline_manual_18.

Weidner, C. K., II, & Purohit, Y. S. (2009). When power has leaders: Some indicators of power-addiction among organizational leaders. *Journal of Organizational Culture, Communications and Conflict, 13*(1), 83–99.

White, A. (2004). Environmental harms, causation, and act utilitarianism. *Environmental Ethics, 26*(2), 189–203.

White, R. W. (1959). Motivation reconsidered: The concept of competence. *Psychological Review, 66*(5), 297–333.

Wicklund, R. A., & Gollwitzer, P. M. (1981). Symbolic self-completion, attempted influence, and self-deprecation. *Basic and Applied Social Psychology, 2*(2), 89–114.

Wicklund, R. A., & Gollwitzer, P. M. (2013). *Symbolic self-completion.* New York: Routledge.

Wilde, J. A., & Finkelstein, J. H. (2022). Disgraced presidents shouldn't get tenure: Why enrich someone whose career ended in controversy? *The Chronicle of Higher Education,* November 13. www.chronicle.com/article/ disgraced-presidents-shouldnt-get-tenure?cid=gen_sign_in.

Wilson, A. T. (2018). Honesty as a virtue. *Metaphilosophy, 49*(3), 262–280.

Wilson, B. (1953). *Twelve steps and twelve traditions.* New York: Alcoholics Anonymous Press.

Wodak, R. (2017). The "Establishment," the "Élites," and the "People": Who's who? *Journal of Language and Politics, 16*(4), 551–565.

Wood, A. M., Froh, J. J., & Geraghty, A. W. (2010). Gratitude and well-being: A review and theoretical integration. *Clinical Psychology Review, 30*(7), 890–905.

Worthington, E. L, & Allison, S. T. (2018). *Heroic humility: What the science of humility can say to people raised on self-focus.* Washington, DC: American Psychological Association.

Worthington, E. L., Davis, D. E., & Hook, J. N. (2017). *Handbook of humility.* New York: Routledge.

Wu, I. H., Williams, M., Crawford, E., & Chiao, Y. C. (2020). Exploring the daily relationship between envy and well-being through envy-coping behaviors at work. *Academy of Management, 2020*(1), 12427.

Xu, F., Xu, B., Anderson, V., & Caldwell, C. (2019). Humility as enlightened leadership: A Chinese perspective. *Journal of Management Development*, *38*(3), 158–174.

Yip, J., & Walker, D. O. H. (2022). Leaders mentoring others: The effects of implicit followership theory on leader integrity and mentoring. *The International Journal of Human Resource Management*, *33*(13), 2688–2718.

Zhang, X., Tian, G., Ma, C. et al. (2020). "Too much of a good thing?": Exploring the dark side of empowering leadership by linking it with unethical pro-organizational behavior. *Leadership & Organization Development Journal*, *42*(1), 32–46.

Leadership

Ronald Riggio
Claremont Mckenna College

Ronald E. Riggio, Ph.D. is the Henry R. Kravis Professor of Leadership and Organisational Psychology and former Director of the Kravis Leadership Institute at Claremont McKenna College. Dr. Riggio is a psychologist and leadership scholar with over a dozen authored or edited books and more than 150 articles/book chapters. He has worked as a consultant, and serves on multiple editorial boards.

Susan Murphy
University of Edinburgh

Susan E. Murphy is Chair in Leadership Development at the University of Edinburgh Business School. She has published numerous articles and book chapters on leadership, leadership development, and mentoring. Susan was formerly Director of the School of Strategic Leadership Studies at James Madison University and Professor of Leadership Studies. Prior to that, she served as faculty and associate director of the Henry R. Kravis Leadership Institute at Claremont McKenna College. She also serves on the editorial board of The Leadership Quarterly.

Georgia Sorenson
University of Cambridge

The late Georgia Sorenson, Ph.D. was the James MacGregor Burns Leadership Scholar at the Moller Institute and Moller By-Fellow of Churchill College at Cambridge University. Before coming to Cambridge, she founded the James MacGregor Burns Academy of Leadership at the University of Maryland, where she was Distinguished Research Professor. An architect of the leadership studies field, Dr. Sorenson has authored numerous books and refereed journal articles.

Advisory Board

Micha Popper, *University of Haifa*
Terry Price, *University of Richmond*
Krish Raval, *University of Oxford*
Roni Reiter-Palmon, *University of Nebraska*
Birgit Schyns, *Durham University*
Gillian Secrett, *University of Cambridge*
Nicholas Warner, *Claremont McKenna College*

About the Series

Cambridge Elements in Leadership is multi- and inter-disciplinary, and will have broad appeal for leadership courses in Schools of Business, Education, Engineering, Public Policy, and in the Social Sciences and Humanities

Cambridge Elements ≡

Leadership

Elements in the Series

Leadership Studies and the Desire for Shared Agreement
Stan Amaladas

Leading the Future of Technology
Rebecca LaForgia

Cultural Dynamics and Leadership
Nathan W. Harter

Leading for Innovation: Leadership Actions to Enhance Follower Creativity
Michael D Mumford

There Is More Than One Way To Lead: The Charismatic, Ideological, And Pragmatic (CIP) Theory Of Leadership
Samuel T. Hunter, Jeffrey B. Lovelace

The Hazards of Great Leadership: Detrimental Consequences of Leader Exceptionalism
James K. Beggan, Scott T. Allison, and George R. Goethals

A full series listing is available at: www.cambridge.org/CELE

Printed in the United States
by Baker & Taylor Publisher Services